A GIFT FOR

Wendy DeRoche

❖ FROM ❖

Bill DeRoche

Creating a Charmed Life

CREATING A
CHARMED LIFE

VICTORIA MORAN

BOOKS

HarperSanFrancisco

BOK 3008

Published under license from HarperCollins Publishers, Inc.

HarperCollins®, ▉®, and HarperSanFrancisco™ are trademarks of HarperCollins Publishers Inc.

Designed by Joseph Rutt

The Library of Congress has cataloged the original edition of this title as follows:
Moran, Victoria
Creating a charmed life: sensible, spiritual secrets every busy woman should know / Victoria Moran. — 1st ed.
p.   cm.
ISBN 0–06–251580–2(pbk.)
1. Women—Conduct of life.   I. Title.
BJ1610.M65   1999
158.1'28'082—dc21   98–55302

ISBN 0-06-095478-7 (Hallmark edition)

00 01 02 03 RRD 10 9 8 7 6 5

Table of Contents

Acknowledgments

Thanks first to my agent, Patti Breitman, for being behind this book from start to finish, as well as for being a helpful mentor and cherished friend. I also wish to thank my insightful editor, Liz Perle, as well as Diane Gedymin, Caroline Pincus, David Hennessy, Rosana Francescato, Terri Leonard, Margery Buchanan, Meg Lenihan, Amy Durgan, Joe Rutt, and everyone else at Harper San Francisco whose work and vision directly resulted in *Creating a Charmed Life*. Appreciation goes as well to Dr. Richard Carlson for his generous foreword.

Thanks for assistance, encouragement, and wise words to Barbara Bartocci, Liz Brown, Rev. Karyn Bradley, Tess Brubeck, Sheree Bykofsky, Kris Carlson, Alma Chapin, Martha Childers, Terah Kathryn Collins, Maril Crabtree, Elizabeth Cutting, JoLee Fishback, Linda Flake, Lidia Garbach-Young, Jacqee Gafford, Denise Goss, Frankie Grady, Halaine Guidry, Suzanne Hatlestad, Beth Ingram, Trena Keating, Karen Kelly, Crystal Leaman, Gary Lemm, Nancy Lowry, Betty Melton, Siãn Melton, Talane Miedaner, Rita Moran, Robert Morris, Sherry Payne, Toni Rader, Jill Reynolds, Rita Rousseau, Pete Shiflett, Barbara Shapiro, Deborah Shouse, LouAnn Stahl, Paula Switzer, David

Timmons, Kristi Tucker, Gaile Varnum, Maureen Waters, Carol Wiesner, and Ann Wylie.

For special help on this project, I wish to acknowledge my daughter, Rachael Adair Moran, whose working title motivated me to turn an idea into a book, and who inspires me every day as I see her creating her uniquely charmed life; my mother, Gladys Marshall, for input on several of the "secrets" and for bequeathing me the writing gene; and the late Adelene (Dede) DeSoto, who first shared with me the spiritual tools for creating a charmed life. To my husband, William Melton: thank you more than I can say for your insights, your patience, and your love.

Foreword
by Richard Carlson

To be quite honest, my only hesitation in writing this foreword was that—you guessed it—I'm a man! After all, I thought, "How could I write an appropriate foreword to a book geared exclusively toward women?" Then I said to myself, "What an honor—I must have a charmed life."

It is my privilege to introduce this beautiful and important book to you. Indeed, part of my charmed life includes being a friend and colleague of Victoria Moran—one of the most sincere, wise, and kind human beings I've ever had the privilege of knowing.

When I first met Victoria, I was impressed with her seemingly effortless way of life. I don't mean to imply that she doesn't work hard, or that she doesn't have her share of difficult challenges—she most certainly does. Yet, there was something about her—something that made life seem so simple, as if her life were somehow charmed. I've since learned that her life is indeed charmed, not because of any easy-street set of circumstances, but rather entirely as a result of her own efforts.

As we have spoken over the years, the reasons for this charmed-life feeling have become clear. Above all, I believe, is the way she shapes and molds her experience in a positive direction. But, it's far deeper than merely putting a positive slant on her life. It's more the way she transforms ordinary life into a set of extraordinary experiences, taking simple day-to-day opportunities and somehow turning them into almost magical episodes. She is able to turn something that most people would consider a hassle into an incredible and insightful learning experience. Or, in a realistic way, she's somehow able to find, in the midst of a hectic day, a way of feeling peace. If you give her ten minutes, she'll invariably find a way to make those few moments seem like a haven of relaxation.

In this book you'll be rewarded with dozens of powerful and practical strategies that will help you bring out the "charmed" in your own life. Through your reading you'll see new ways to nourish yourself, improve your attitude, become more effective and loving, appreciate your life, relax, and make everything seem a little easier.

I know that Victoria wrote this book for women, but I have to say that, even as a man, I loved every page and appreciated its application to my own life. It also helped me to better understand the ways that I might support my wife, Kris, and our two daughters as they enhance their own charmed ways.

Like Victoria, I believe I have a charmed life. With few exceptions, I wake up each morning thanking God for yet another day and wondering what interesting events and challenges will be unfolding. I've learned that having a charmed life involves making lots and lots of charmed choices and engaging in positive, life- and love-affirming habits. Without question, this book will guide you in that direction.

I hope you savor this book over and over again. It contains simple wisdom, put forth in a beautiful series of essays. Good luck, and may your life become charmed!

Introduction

We usually think of a charmed life as one somebody else gets to live. But I know for a fact that you can construct for yourself a life in which serendipity is commonplace and things go right an extraordinary percentage of the time. *Creating a Charmed Life* is a guide to doing just that. My intention in writing it is to bring charmed living out of its country-club-like, members-only status and make it instead a viable option for anyone willing to do the work.

This applies to both men and women, of course. I've written this book for women because I know firsthand about creating a charmed life as a female—and about the multiple demands placed on women today, demands that can crowd the pursuit of a charmed life right off the priority list. Every woman deserves to know that her passions count for something. She also deserves ample time to pursue them.

Still, since universal truths underlie the suggestions that follow, they are not all gender-specific. You can share many of them with your husband, your beau, or your brother, as well as your mom and your best friend. That way, you'll not only be creating a charmed life—you'll have people around you to support it, people who are taking steps toward their own charmed lives.

Let me give you some background on how this book came to be. I believed early on that I lived a charmed life—sort of. Extraordinary experiences, primarily involving travel and meeting famous people, densely populated my childhood and youth. But I also disliked myself, struggled with an eating disorder, and had a list of fears eighty-three entries long.

At times I resigned myself to believing that the struggles were the price of the sparkle. I see in retrospect that the sparkle was the result of the charmed living principles I then knew and practiced. Many of those I learned in childhood came from Dede, the remarkable elderly woman who helped raise me. Her conversation was peppered with references to Emerson, the Bible, and pithy proverbs she would invariably introduce with the words "There's an old saying . . ." My struggles, on the other hand, came largely from not knowing more of those living principles.

I've spent my adult life on a quest for the missing pieces. It's taken me as far away as Tibet and India and brought me home again to Dede's New Testament and Emerson's essays. What I'm offering you on the pages that follow is what I've learned. I certainly don't practice all of this all the time, but even an imperfect application of wisdom, whether a folksy how-to or a spiritual gem, can transform something as mutable as a woman's life.

You start where you are to get your life where you want it, whether it seems to be liberally charmed already or far from it. You don't need any more time, money, or inspiration than it took to pick up this book. The ideas we'll explore are both sensible and spiritual. When you put spiritual concepts to practical use, you have a combination that works to change your reality and charm your life.

Creating a Charmed Life

1.

CREATE A CHARMED LIFE

Just as it's easier for little children to learn to write if they have some big, fat pencils, it's easier to create a charmed life if you have some big, fat dreams.

In fairy tales, being charmed was the opposite of being cursed. Nowadays, we're not supposed to believe in either one of those, and yet we do. We give credence to cursedness every time we say, "Wouldn't you know it?" and "I knew it was too good to be true." We believe in charmed lives, too—for example, when somebody else gets the private office, moves to an apartment with a river view, and then marries a guy who strongly resembles Sir Lancelot. It's enough to make us think that some women have fairy godmothers working overtime while ours have taken early retirement.

The facts, however, belie the superstition. People who seem to lead charmed lives do not have a magical assistant, and they're no better or brighter than anybody else. They have simply put into practice, knowingly or not, the attitudes, aptitudes, and propensities that orchestrate harmonious circumstances.

If you learn these when you're young, you get a head start. But you can learn them later, enjoy the benefits just as much, and probably appreciate them more. Regardless of when you discover these precepts, implementing them will create your charmed life—one that is rich, full, meaningful, *and* manageable. Here's how you can begin:

Look at the wonders that are in your experience already. Where have you come from? What are you proud of? What can you do? What have you seen? Whom have you helped? What amazing human beings have chosen to be your friends, your mate, your children? This is your working capital. Be aware of it and grateful for it. There is little sadder than a person who has ample makings for a charmed life but just won't see it.

Next, think about your days the way they are now. How much of your time, effort, and attention go toward succeeding where it matters most: with well-nurtured relationships, well-chosen experiences, and well-tended aspirations? Putting emphasis here is not popular; it seems too real and too risky for the faint of heart. Nevertheless, it calls for only a shift in priorities, not a day with more hours in it. That's because you create a charmed life by doing only a few things you aren't doing already. You get the time to do them (and some time to spare) by eliminating from your life what isn't serving you. Then you do what's left with unmistakable style.

Finally, decide what the life you want looks like. This is just an idea. You're not pouring concrete, and you can change how you see your ideal life whenever you like. Don't edit yourself at this point. Just as it's easier for little children to learn to write if they have some big, fat pencils, it's easier to create a charmed life if you have some big, fat dreams.

Don't worry if your dreams seem impractical or if they're replete with contradiction. Deborah Shouse, a wonderful writer friend of mine, described her paradoxical vision in the form of a childhood memory: "I wanted to walk on the sand and leave no trace, yet I wanted to build a sand castle and make my mark." In the realm of charmed lives, this is both possible and plausible, because creating a charmed life is, at its foundation, spiritual. Although it has aspects as mundane as making the bed (see Secret 51), the basis for living splendidly is a growing conviction that you are here for a reason, a purpose. What we're calling a charmed life is the life you were meant to live, the one in which it is perfectly acceptable to want the moon, as long as you're willing to get over your fear of flying.

2.

FOLLOW YOUR HEART

*Accomplishing your daily goals has a place, but the heart
has a valid agenda of its own. When you can look back on a
day and find within it even one warm memory or a single
touching story, you've paid attention to your heart.*

There are all sorts of pragmatic, real-world reasons why women
today are pushed for time and starved for serenity. The hours we
spend each day at work, in the car, with our partners, with our
kids, and with our hundred and one other commitments can feel
as if they added up to well over twenty-four. To live a charmed
life, we have to retrieve some sanity from all the confusion, state
our priorities, and have the courage to believe in ourselves and
our dreams.

Beyond all that, however, looms the number-one reason so
many women are hurried, stressed, and frantic: our society
demands that we live from our heads, while our instincts insist
that we follow our hearts.

I saw this in my own life one Friday morning when I was
behind on everything. My husband's three children, who are with
us only part of the time, were over for a long weekend. When
they're here, I want desperately to re-create *The Brady Bunch* for
them and my teenage daughter. Unlike Mrs. Brady, however, I
had a writing assignment due that I'd meant to finish the day
before. And we were out of cereal and cat litter and double-A bat-

teries. To top it off, I was fighting the flu. I wanted to call in sick, but since I work for myself there wasn't anybody I could call.

As I was pondering how to meet the divergent needs of four kids, an editor, and an immune system, my daughter and step-daughter came in from outside bearing a pigeon with a broken wing. "It's bleeding," they said repeatedly, to be sure I was aware of the gravity of the situation. My first internal response was strictly head stuff: "Oh—shall we say—shucks! This is not the day I need this. . . . If I had time to take somebody to a doctor, I'd be taking myself. . . . There's a bleeding pigeon wrapped in a coat that has to be dry cleaned. . . . And why does every injured creature in the Midwest find its way to this house? Do the chipmunks make maps?"

But even as my head cataloged these assorted miseries, I'd begun to act from my heart, from my natural self, who would have picked up that pigeon just like the girls did. I put the bird in a closet away from our dog and the cats and then called the one veterinarian I know who has enough heart himself to take on the unprofitable task of treating wild pigeons. He said he could see us at noon.

I shifted into heart mode and made a run to the quick mart. When I got back and settled in to write, it was with more focus than I'd had in days. The work I expected to take several hours was finished before we left for the animal hospital. At the same time, I felt a surge of energy and knew that whether I ended up with a bout of flu or not, it wasn't going to happen before taking care of the bird. My heart would see to that.

Sadly, the vet was not able to save the pigeon, but the pigeon saved me. I remembered that day that, as is true for most women, my heart is first concerned with sustaining, supporting, and empowering life, whether by fixing a healthy dinner at home, presenting a humane solution at the office, or rearranging a schedule to accommodate a person—or a pigeon—in need.

Accomplishing your daily goals has a place, but the heart has a valid agenda of its own. When you can look back on a day and find within it even one warm memory or a single touching story, you've paid attention to your heart. That's worth whatever time it took.

3.

GET AMPLE SHINE TIME

Everybody needs some time to shine. . . .
Nobody is in the spotlight nonstop.
Accept that you will shine, step back, then shine again.
The moon has phases from dark to full. So do we.

Everybody needs some time to shine, time to be recognized, special, admired. It's not selfish; it's human.

Early one Saturday I saw in the local paper that a workshop for blues musicians was scheduled for that very morning. I showed the notice to my husband, who intends to be the world's next great blues harmonica player. "I'd like to go," he said, "but I promised I would paint your office." I assured him that the office could wait and sent him off with my blessing.

He thought I was being selfless and wonderful, but I really wasn't. You see, I'd had a lot of shine time that week—a couple of career successes, a lunch out with five favorite friends, and a massage that accounted for one, entire, luxurious hour. I was full. When you're basking in the sun, it's natural to want those you love to join you there. But if you're not getting enough of your own shine time, it's easy to be needy, whiny, and pitiful.

It can get worse than that: the shine-deficient tend to resent other people's accomplishments and dampen their dreams. Sometimes, they sabotage the potential of even their own children because their need for personal recognition is so seldom met. Parents who want to keep their children from pursuing an art or a sport "because it's not practical" are in this category. So are those who push their kids toward unrealistic academic or athletic achievements. They're trying to get some shine secondhand.

For your own benefit as well as for the benefit of those around you, shining regularly is as crucial as bathing regularly. You can get the shine time that's essential to creating a charmed life in myriad ways. Among them are the following:

Indulge yourself often in what you do well. If you're a good swimmer, swim. If you're a good seamstress, sew.

Spend time with people who think you're splendid and who tell you so.

Celebrate yourself. Mark the occasions of your life with friends and festivity. Never get too old to have birthdays.

Train those close to you to appreciate shine time by giving them some. Keep track of their special days. Notice their accomplishments. Never leave an honest compliment unspoken.

Don't downplay your successes ("It was just an automatic promotion; anybody would have gotten it").

When you're in the limelight, invite others to share it. Think of Academy Award recipients thanking all those people by name.

When the world isn't noticing you, notice yourself. Buy yourself a present. Send yourself flowers. Take yourself to lunch someplace that uses cloth napkins.

Allow other people unimpeded shine time. We like to look at celebrities and make comments like "Nobody is worth that much money" and "Why doesn't somebody teach that woman how to dress?" Just for practice, at least some of the time, let it go. Let other people shine, even the radiant strangers on TV.

Welcome shine time as a cyclic occurrence. Nobody is in the spotlight nonstop. Accept that you will shine, step back, then shine again. The moon has phases from dark to full. So do we. We're fully valuable throughout the cycle. At certain times, we just attract more attention.

4.

PLAY YOUR FREE SQUARE

*We can use, trade, barter, and build on the assets that are
inherently ours to flesh out our lives with other good
things that don't come so easily.*

In the game of Bingo, every player starts with a bonus: the free
square in the middle. Because everybody gets one, nobody thinks
much of it, but the free square is just as valuable in winning the
game as B–7 or O–69.

We have "free squares" in our lives, too: talents, abilities, and
inexplicable aptitudes that make certain things almost effortless.
Maybe we can sing, or we're good at math, or children warm to
us and listen when we talk. But when someone comments on our
free square, we tend to say, "Oh, that. It's nothing." Because we
didn't work hard to get it, the same way a player doesn't have to
perform to get a free square on the Bingo card, we undervalue
what may be our most serviceable attribute.

Without the benefit of our free square—or squares: you can
certainly have more than one—we run ourselves ragged trying to
be something we aren't. We work diligently to fit our round pegs
into square holes, or to fit our round selves into the media's angu-
lar ideal. When we recognize and appreciate our own free squares,
though, we can see that the key to our success and fulfillment is
inside the person we are, not the one we think we're supposed to
be. We can use, trade, barter, and build on the assets that are

inherently ours to flesh out our lives with other good things that don't come so easily.

If you're unclear about your own free squares, answer the following questions: Is there an area of your life—even one you may have regarded as insignificant—in which good things tend to happen repeatedly and automatically? Do you have an aptitude for something that seems so natural you can't understand why other people struggle with it? What do you get compliments about? How would you finish the sentence, "I've just got a knack for..."

Your answers may indicate that you, like my daughter Rachael, have a free square for money. This child has always had an affinity for cash, both acquiring it and hanging onto it. When she was only three, she once interrupted a grown-up financial discussion to say, "If I had a savings account that was drawing interest, I could make you a loan."

Or, like me, you may have a free square for meeting people. I constantly run into people who are helpful, fascinating, and sometimes famous. I meet them on buses, in cafés, riding elevators. It just happens.

Perhaps you, like my friend Francesca, have an uncanny penchant for winning things. Since I've known her, she's won a fax machine, a Ford Escort, and a trip to Disney World. What she doesn't win, she can usually get wholesale.

Once you identify your free squares, play them by using what's easy to help you with what isn't. When Francesca won that fax machine, for instance, she had been unsuccessfully looking for work for several weeks. She thought about selling her prize—she could have used the money—but Francesca is a woman who takes her free squares seriously. She decided that the universe wouldn't have supplied her with this techno-toy if she wasn't supposed to use it. To try the thing out and see how it worked, she faxed her resume to some personnel directors. Her top pick responded and hired her.

The next time you think you might not have what it takes to get the kind of life you're after, enlist the help of your free square. Your particular gift may not look like what you need at the moment; Francesca's fax machine didn't look like a job offer either. Use your free square. Let it work for you. Be proud of it and grateful for it. Bingo!

5.

TAKE TEN

*Even if your busyness tells you that you can't afford to
take quiet time, know that you can't afford not to.*

A lot of women are juggling a job, a husband, and kids. Or a job, an ex-husband, and kids. Some are working eighty-hour weeks and getting those notices from the dry cleaner warning that if they don't pick it up soon, their favorite jacket is going to Goodwill Industries. It doesn't leave much time for a spiritual life, and without one, a charmed life is pretty tough to come by.

Taking some soul time every day is the antidote for the beleaguered, whether the source of the strain is work, family, inner emptiness, or some combination of those. Attention given to the spirit produces energy instead of only consuming it. That's what people who are actively aware of this deeper dimension have in common: an energy source that doesn't run out.

The surest way to access this energy source is through silence, through taking a specified amount of time each day for meditation, prayer, journal writing (see Secret 50), or inspirational reading. Some proponents of meditation guarantee inner peace if you spend an hour a day in purposeful quiet; others recommend twenty minutes morning and evening. It always seemed to me that if you had that much time to spare, you'd have a pretty peaceful life even without meditating.

It was my friend Elizabeth who taught me the importance of getting my silence in the time I could give it. When Elizabeth was in her twenties, she was fresh out of Northwestern with an MBA and in search of a worldview that worked. She had given up her childhood religion and hadn't found a suitable replacement. The work world seemed harsher than the academic one, and despite the letters after her name, she faced it with some trepidation.

She shared these concerns with her father—who now seemed considerably wiser than he had when she left home at eighteen—and he offered her a quotation from an old book of spiritual teachings, *The Secret of the Golden Flower:* "If you will be quiet but ten minutes a day, it will save countless lives and a thousand aeons. If you do not, the light streams out, I know not wither." She took the advice and used those ten minutes as her touchstone while she explored the myriad options before her. That was fifteen years ago, but taking the advice gave her such direction that she can still recite the passage verbatim.

Whatever it takes to skim from each day ten minutes of silence, make it your highest priority. You can be creative to get the time: Set your clock a little earlier than your housemates', stay at the office ten minutes after everyone else has gone, or slip into a church on your walk home from work and take that transformative sliver of time for yourself.

Even if your busyness tells you that you can't afford to take quiet time, know that you can't afford not to. To be sure I get some of it every morning, I light the candle on my nightstand as soon as I awaken. (It's a vanilla candle, by the way; life is too short to burn candles that don't smell nice.) When I get back from the shower and my ego is listing all the important things I have to do, the candle seems to say, "C'mon, you've got ten minutes." When I take those minutes, some of their calmness and clarity stays with me. The day takes on a grace and ease that I didn't have to earn. I just get to enjoy it.

6.

PRACTICE THE
VACATION PRINCIPLE

Regard your life as an extended working vacation. . . .
Be a tourist in your hometown and your own life.

When you're a tourist, the place you are is the most important place there is. It was like that when Sheree Bykofsky, a literary agent from New York, visited me in Kansas City, where she was attending a writers' conference. She's traveled a lot, but as I drove her through my neighborhood she was like a second-grader on her first field trip. Everything was fascinating. She snapped pictures of my house, my husband, my neighbor's puppy. I took her to the local quick mart for more film. She took pictures of the businesses: Prospero's Books, Muddy's Coffee House, Revue Vintage Clothing.

She wrote later and said, "I just loved Kansas City." I believe she did. I also believe that someone with Sheree's ability to live fully in the time and place at hand would be equally enamored of Cincinnati or Charlottesville or Spokane. People like this are so full of life that they discover the liveliness around them wherever they are. They exemplify one of the secrets of a charmed life: the vacation principle.

Once you get it, you live as if you were always on vacation, savoring every minute and collecting memories like snapshots.

Relaxing and having fun become priorities. You have more patience for standing in line, getting lost, and paying full price. You can be enraptured by something that would ordinarily be of minimal interest: a museum, a cathedral, a grave site, or a guy dressed like a giant mouse. It's because you've put yourself in absorption mode: you're on vacation and you expect to find things intriguing.

Wake up! You *are* on vacation. You won't be here forever. When you comprehend that, you'll categorize infinitely more of life's offerings as "not to be missed." You may find yourself having a first-time hankering to visit the museums and cathedrals in your own city. An adult education catalog might look like a ticket to bliss.

When you internalize the vacation principle, you will notice increased vibrancy around you. Colors will seem more vivid, sounds clearer, scents easier to detect and differentiate. This happens because you're paying close attention to all that's going on. Your memory is apt to improve, because you will find more images worth holding on to. Your energy level will rise because you're being stimulated by your interests, your passions, your fascinations.

Regard your life as an extended working vacation. Find nooks and crannies to explore, side streets to meander, beaches to walk along. Stop at a scenic overlook. Speak another language. Ride a carousel. Be a tourist in your hometown and your own life. When you do this, even the lackluster aspects of living day to day can seem like part of an amazing journey.

Employ the vacation principle when you're feeling sorry for yourself because you haven't gotten your way. If you are figuratively in the Poconos when you were hoping for Paris, you're still on vacation. You can still have a terrific time, and Paris will always be there. This attitude grows in usefulness as your life gets better. With the vacation principle in play, you won't have to hang on to every glistening experience as if you'll never have another. You can let each go in its time, knowing others are on their way. They will be different from one another—as different as the Pyramids are from the Bahamas, or the Great Wall from the Grand Canyon. Each one can give you glorious memories.

7

CONSERVE YOUR ENERGY

*Ridding your life of the most egregious energy thieves
makes you a prime candidate for getting tired for
all the right reasons.*

Almost every woman I know is either a little tired or flat-out exhausted. It seems to me that the main cause of this physical and mental fatigue is our incessant attempt to fill in for Atlas. We feel responsible for so many people and tasks that it does seem that we're balancing the world on our shoulders. This makes us weary before we even do anything. Certainly we have responsibilities, but feeling overly responsible for our clients, our spouses, or even our children can deplete us unnecessarily.

During a turbulent airplane flight when my daughter, Rachael, was a preschooler, I sought to comfort her by saying, "It's okay, Honey: we're together." She looked at me solemnly and said, "I'd rather be by myself and alive." I had to stifle laughter, but the lesson was clear: in even my most responsible position, I am not indispensable.

Getting a realistic view of your responsibility level can be the first step in personal energy conservation. It allows you to be aware of and minimize these six energy-eroding habits:

Talking too much. Conversation can be stimulating, educational, therapeutic, and bonding, but we drain ourselves by chattering about minutia. My *nana* used to tell me that every phrase uttered should have to pass three gatekeepers. The first asks, "Is it true?" The second, "Is it necessary?" The third, "Is it kind?" When I remember that, I talk less and say more.

Sleep deprivation. Researchers say that most adults are sleep-starved. Our boundless caffeine consumption supports this contention. According to the Indian medical system of Ayurveda, people who train themselves to go to bed by 10:00 awaken early, refreshed, and energized. It's worth a try.

Unrealistic expectations. Attempting to have a house as clean as your mother's, a body as lean as a model's, and a bank balance as hefty as a mogul's would exhaust anybody. Moderation makes more sense. If you consistently clean on Saturdays, exercise three mornings a week, and stay out of debt, your home, your figure, and your finances should be just fine.

The integrity gap. Bridging the gap between who we are and how we wish to appear requires considerable effort. It is a major drain to say one thing and do another. "Walk your talk" didn't get to be a cliché for nothing.

Gossip. Getting to feel superior ("I can't believe she did that") and being part of a supposed confidence ("Of course I won't tell anybody") is not only unkind, it also takes more energy than most of us have to spare. Keeping the information, whether actual or fabricated, in mental storage compounds the burden. The phrase "carrying tales" is telling because you really do have to carry them—and hide them, worry about them, and keep track of them, too.

Preaching. Peddling our philosophic wares at every opportunity is both a great way to become an insufferable bore and a direct route to burnout. When what you believe or practice changes your life, others will notice. Then they'll ask to know more—or your actions will speak so eloquently that you won't have to say a word.

Ridding your life of the most egregious energy thieves makes you a prime candidate for getting tired for all the right reasons. Healthy physical activity is the most obvious. But you also will not have yawned in vain if you're bushed from doing the work, sustaining the relationships, and diving into the experiences that give your life its identity and impetus. This kind of fatigue is appropriate and curable. Take a hot bath. Get a good night's sleep. And buy another box of candles: it's okay every so often to burn one at both ends.

8.

GIVE UP YOUR
MOUNTAIN

*If you're looking for a charmed life, or even just a ray of
hope, you first have to recognize the mountain that is
most effectively blocking your way.*

The primary obstacle between you and a charmed life is your mountain. Your mountain is the issue that seems foreboding, daunting, overwhelming. This is no ordinary challenge. It is the difficulty that seems to be standing in the way of all you want to do, the problem that, if solved, would free you to be everything you were created to be.

Your mountain might be an addiction—yours or that of someone you love. Being short on cash and long on debt can be the makings of a mountain. So can the education you never got, the man you never married, or the baby you never had. A chronic illness or disability can bear a striking resemblance to Everest; so can an unfortunate childhood that is historically over but alive every day within you.

The fascinating aspect of these mountains, I think, is that they're subjective geology. That is, the same situation one woman readily triumphs over and grows beyond can keep someone else snowed in at base camp for years. And the person who effortlessly scaled that particular peak can be defeated by one that looks half its size.

I learned about mountains as a compulsive overeater. Although my last binge was years ago, I clearly remember how impossible it was to avoid food I didn't need once it occurred to me that there were leftovers in the fridge or ice cream on the planet. Once I embraced a spiritual program of recovery, I realized that food was never really the mountain I'd thought it was. It was simply the most visible area in my life at the time that I had refused to give to God.

With this understanding, I should have gotten out of the mountain-climbing business. I didn't. I chose instead to create other mountains. After I was widowed in my thirties, I erected the mountain of "I am all alone in the world and no one will ever marry me." I made the best life I could in the foothills of that one for several years. It was only after I made peace with my singlehood that I met my second husband.

As we were setting up housekeeping, I found myself again creating mountain-making apparatus. Money seemed appropriate. I have the erratic income of an author and speaker, and between my husband and me we have four kids counting on college. This was a mountain made in heaven.

Thankfully, I was working intensively at the time with a couple of overeaters. In hearing these two recount their struggles with sweets, buffets, and fast-food emporia—my own one-time nemeses—I realized that all three of us had made mountains, and we'd made them too big for our climbing abilities. It's these self-constructed alps we really must surrender.

If your belief system includes a personal God, let Him or Her or It take on this thing that has defied your best shots. "Turning it over" is a skill as necessary for living as for making pancakes. If God isn't a comfortable concept for you, work with turning your mountain over to the process of life itself, remembering how exquisitely even the most baffling situations often play out.

Such surrender is no small feat in a culture that applauds the strong, the independent, and the self-sufficient. That heroic stuff is fine when the problem is something we can handle through our own strong, independent self-sufficiency. But nobody climbs a mountain alone.

If you're looking for a charmed life, or even just a ray of hope, you first have to recognize the mountain that is most effectively blocking your way. Then you have to be willing to let it be there—tall, pristine, and unconquered by you. You have to be willing to let God (or whatever name you wish to give a Power greater than your mountain) deal with it.

This doesn't mean that you go to bed and wait. Your critical task at this point is to do what needs to be done to keep your life on track in spite of the fact that there is a mountain outside your door. The new rules are these: God takes care of the mountain; you take care of your life. Make breakfast. Go to work. Renew your driver's license. Take your mother-in-law to her doctor's appointment. Call your honey and tell him you'll meet him for dinner at that romantic little Italian place.

And while you're living your life, committed to making the best one you can with the available ingredients, your mountain may start to erode, or you may feel that you've been lifted over it. You might get climbing lessons and a dozen Sherpas to help on your ascent. However the particulars play out, you will no longer be focused on this enormous obstacle. The problem existed—in some cases, it may still exist—but it's not a mountain anymore. It's a road, and it leads to your charmed life.

9.

COEXIST GRACEFULLY
WITH THE UNRESOLVED

*We build the courage to get through the substantial trials
by learning to cohabit serenely with the trivia.*

Some years ago, a friend of mine attended meetings of Emotions Anonymous. She learned much of value there, but in particular a single concept, that of living at peace with unsolved problems. Every person known for her poise, grace, and equanimity has figured out a way to do this.

The ability to coexist with the unresolved has immense practical value. Without it, we can function at our best only when everything is perfect (in other words, never). Even solvable problems seldom have instant answers. Until these problems are worked through, we share space with them.

Most of the unresolved irritations we have to live with are simply that: irritations. Maybe you get a letter from the bank saying you've bounced a check. You're sure it's a bank error—well, pretty sure—but it's Friday evening and you can't do anything about it until Monday. Or your best friend thinks you gossiped about her and she isn't speaking to you. If she would tell you what you supposedly said, you'd have a chance to plead your innocence, but she's not returning your calls.

Occasionally we have to coexist with something serious. A suspicious mammogram, for instance, means waiting for a biopsy, then waiting for the results. It can be agonizing to live in the limbo of not knowing about our own health or safety or that of someone we love. We build the courage to get through the substantial trials by learning to cohabit serenely with the trivia.

A charmed life is one that is lived fully during both smooth times and rough ones. To help do this, remember:

There will always be something to work on, something that could be better. If you wake up one morning and there is nothing to deal with, your address has probably become Forest Lawn.

You are not "in denial" when you recognize a problem and behave normally in spite of it. That's the difference between having a problem *in* your life and making a problem *of* your life.

Dilemmas need fences to prevent them from migrating. Fencing in an obstacle means keeping it contained so it doesn't affect the rest of your life. An example might be keeping a minor job problem at the office instead of bringing it to dinner and to bed. When you have well-tended fences, one or two or a dozen things going wrong won't negate the 147 that are going right.

When you're met with a situation that can't be solved right away, do what you can to coexist with it. Talk about it with someone you trust. Write about it in your journal, even if you just write "This isn't fair!" in kindergarten-sized letters over and over again.

Give yourself ten minutes or half an hour to be actively angry, frightened, or both.

Then take whatever action toward resolution you reasonably can, and give each action session a definitive ending, the way dessert ends a meal or a period ends a sentence. This can be as simple as telling another person "I've done all I can do on this for now." Then stop. Read. Take a walk. Take a shower. It's no small thing to attend to your life in general when everything in you wants to obsess over some nagging particular. But as Rudolph Nureyev once said of ballet, "It never becomes easy. It does become possible."

10.

INVITE ADVENTURE

A charmed life is an exuberant life. You get one by loosening up, lightening up, and inviting in stimulating events and people.

As a culture, we are aching for adventure. To find it, some people go in for daredevil sports, while others opt for roller coasters, haunted houses, and action flicks. Still others find adventure by making their lives into do-it-yourself soap operas. They get into dead-end relationships, engage in careless spending, create arguments out of nothing, or make a selection or two from the cafeteria of addictions.

Our adventure deficit has come about because we have made our lives, on the surface at least, sleepily sheltered. Central heat, central air, and thermal windows keep us comfy. Alarm systems, retirement plans, air bags, immunizations, health insurance, house insurance, and—miraculously—*life* insurance are supposed to keep us safe.

In spite of diligently managing so many risks, people are as frightened as ever. It's like playing the carnival game of whacking popping heads with a foam-covered mallet. It feels great to be on a roll—Smack! Zap! Gotcha!—but the heads are set to spring back faster than a mere mortal can keep up with. Because we're trying to whack every possible menace and peril, we focus on menace and peril quite a bit. Since it's terrifying to face them head-on but unrealistic to avoid them completely, many people waffle back and forth between worry and avoidance. Infusing our experience with healthy adventure is a way to make life so interesting we no longer need to borrow trouble, while at the same time increasing our courage a bit so we can better deal with trouble when it does come.

You can usher in a more adventurous life by first surveying your own personality. Some people need a lot of adventure: they're the ones who like to jump out of airplanes. Others need less: just riding in an airplane is plenty. Determine where you fall on the spectrum and look at the way you live to see if you're providing yourself with ample challenges, risks, and opportunities to push your boundaries a bit.

Most of the adventures that garnish charmed lives are small ones: exploring an unfamiliar neighborhood in your own city, auditioning for community theater, or taking a class in a subject that seems fascinating—or one that seems intimidating.

To get some adventure without spending any extra time, simply find adventurous ways to do what you do already. You're going to eat lunch, so why not try a Thai or Ethiopian restaurant instead of one of your usual standbys? Or the next time you're ready to buy a couple of shirts, how about checking out a vintage boutique, a resale shop, an outlet mall, or the fanciest store in town? Where you go isn't important: what makes it an adventure is that it's off your particular beaten path.

And get off your literal beaten path by taking different routes to the places you routinely go, and finding the most interesting way to get somewhere new. I had one of my most memorable adventures while driving back to Missouri after visiting my parents in Florida. I saw a sign on the interstate that said, "New Orleans, 100 miles," followed by a left exit. That was enough of a lure to head south for an unplanned detour. I hadn't realized in doing this that the date was December 31. My daughter and I got to spend New Year's Eve in the incomparable excitement of the French Quarter instead of watching TV at a motel in Little Rock.

A charmed life is an exuberant life. You get one by loosening up, lightening up, and inviting in stimulating events and people. Helen Keller said, "Security is mostly a superstition. . . . Life is either a daring adventure, or nothing." Thank you, Helen.

11.

ACQUIRE DISCRETION

When you are discreet, you protect yourself.
You preserve your honor. You conserve your power.

Discretion is the art of restraint. People who have it do fewer foolish things; when they do behave foolishly, they don't plaster the news on a billboard. Although nearly obliterated in the sixties, discretion is gaining momentum again. That's a good thing, too, because it is indispensable in creating and maintaining a charmed life.

Having discretion doesn't mean being cold and standoffish, or holding feelings inside and allowing them to fester. Discretion simply means keeping your personal life yours and discussing its particulars only with carefully selected confidantes. Sharing, venting, and therapylike encounters have their time and place, but not whenever and wherever the urge hits.

When a woman has discretion, her selfhood is marked by clear boundaries that ask for—and almost always get—respect. Willingness to be open about a painful experience or a worthwhile lesson learned can be a priceless gift to give, but it is possible to share too much of yourself. Synonyms for *open* include *bare, exposed*, and *vulnerable*. Utilizing discretion, you put yourself in this position only with good reason and a little forethought.

Lacking discretion, you might one day realize that you've told everybody you know how much you earn, every injury you've suffered, the details of your sex life, and the sum of your hopes and dreams. This would leave you like a house with all its doors and windows agape. It's open and airy all right, but it's also open to being robbed and flooded.

Discretion seems to come naturally to some people. The rest of us have to learn it, primarily by unlearning the half-truths that have kept it at bay. For starters, discretion is not dishonesty. Just because you don't tell everyone you meet your life story doesn't mean you've betrayed the truth. Let's say the dishwasher repair guy shows up and says, "How are things going?" You could say, "I'm having awful cramps, and my husband and I have been arguing a lot, and I'm really nervous that I might be laid off." Or you could say, "Fine, but the dishwasher leaks." I'm pretty sure you'd still pass a polygraph test.

Furthermore, discretion is not denial. We've been so schooled by the tell-all theories of pop psychology that it's hard to remember that the heart belongs in the chest and not on the sleeve. If in the midst of a career disappointment or grieving the loss of a love, you can appear in public well groomed and in charge of yourself, it doesn't mean you're denying reality. You are instead tapping your inner strength. And the feeling of dignity you'll get as a result will be well deserved.

Less serious situations benefit from discretion as well. You can discreetly refrain from giving a ten-minute explanation every time you decline an invitation or say no to a request. You can keep small talk genuinely small and never have to agonize over having revealed too much to someone you hardly know.

When you are discreet, you protect yourself. You preserve your honor. You conserve your power. You become, in the words of actress Jacqee Gafford, "less a satellite and more a sun."

12.

ENJOY YOUR
ECCENTRICITIES

*It takes a lot of energy to keep parts of yourself under
wraps. Stifle too many of them, and
you risk losing a bit of your soul.*

My favorite teacher—Mrs. Buckley, seventh grade—said that *eccentric* is the word you use for people who are too rich to be called simply crazy. However, Mrs. Buckley seemed pretty eccentric herself. Her classroom was a forum for diverse visitors who had information to impart or axes to grind. Inventors brought their gadgets; politicians brought their platforms; and one frequent guest was determined to get our entire class fluent in Esperanto. Mrs. Buckley herself espoused self-directed learning—as long as we directed ourselves to memorize Keats and Robert Browning. My seventh-grade teacher was an intriguing melange of depth and wisdom and contradictions. I wanted to be just like her.

We all have eccentricities. They don't make us crazy, and we don't have to be rich for them to contribute lavishly to making us who we are. The word *eccentric* comes from geometry and literally means "not having the same center." Our eccentricities are those parts of ourselves that don't fit the familiar pattern.

I know an attorney who is also an opera singer. Some people call her eccentric; others call her fulfilled. The same designations could apply to the carpool mom who tells cliff-hanger stories on the way to school, the waitress who writes a little personal thank-you on the checks, or the businesswoman who passes the time between flights by juggling in the airport. What these women, and Mrs. Buckley, can show the rest of us is how to accept our apparent quirks and capitalize on them.

It takes a lot of energy to keep parts of yourself under wraps. Stifle too many of them, and you risk losing a bit of your soul. If instead of downplaying your more colorful facets, though, you claim them along with your earth-toned parts, you get to be a whole person rather than an easy stereotype. Everyone who gets a label—whether it's "working woman" or "soccer mom"—has infinitely more aspects than that to herself and her life.

In suggesting you enjoy your eccentricities, I am not implying that being "different" is somehow valuable in its own right. It isn't. Each of us, however, has interests and attributes that may not match those of the people around us or fit with the other parts of our own personality. These often include some of our brightest traits. They make us gifted. They make us unique. They make us women to be reckoned with.

Those who believe they are none of these things have usually ignored their most distinctive characteristics because at some time or other those attributes threatened the established order. A family member, a school rule, a boyfriend, a TV commercial—someone or something—gave the message that this gift or talent or preoccupation was unacceptable. The safe retreat was the status quo.

Nobody ever created a charmed life for herself by seeking approval *from* everybody through trying to be *like* everybody.

The catch is that the people who get cloned by their neighbors are usually clones themselves. Because they too are denying their uniqueness, they feel just as unsatisfied as those who seek to emulate them.

If you feel that you left some of your individuality somewhere in your past, or if you can't think of any personal eccentricities that bring you pleasure and pride, I invite you to travel back in memory to age six. What did you want to be? Write it down—not just "teacher" or "ballerina," although certainly write that too, but concentrate on the kind of *person* you wanted to be, the kind of woman you wanted to become. Within that vision is the core of your uniqueness. Find it, and find a place for it in the world you inhabit now.

Whether you unearth the whimsical wonders inside you through this exercise or have been aware of your eccentricities all along, respect them today a little more than usual. Be grateful for them. Enjoy your eccentricities and those of other people. Neutrals have a place, but not as the dominant colors of your life.

13.

ENHANCE YOUR
ENVIRONMENT

Collaborate with nature. Value beauty. Respect your intuitive inklings about the colors, shapes, textures, and patterns that populate your personal world. Create an environment that entices fortune.

If changing your life seems an overwhelming proposition, rearrange your furniture. Your environment—or environments, when you think of your home, your car, your office, and wherever else you spend substantial time—affects your mood and, according to the ancient Chinese teaching of *feng shui*, your fate.

Feng shui is a system for creating pleasing spaces that can relax or energize their inhabitants as needed. The basis of *feng shui* is improving the flow of *chi*, the invisible life energy that acupuncturists work with in healing and that martial artists harness to overpower an opponent. When this energy can flow without impediment, not only does a house feel better, but the lives of the people who live there are said to get better.

When I first learned about *feng shui*, I thought of it as something light and fun—like the generic wisdom inside a fortune cookie. I take it more seriously today because I have repeatedly seen *feng shui* do what it promises: make a difference.

Bookstores carry many books on the subject in their interior-design sections. In addition, there are professional practitioners who will analyze your home or office according to *feng shui* principles and suggest cures for what ails it. For the moment, consider these easy-to-implement, basic tenets:

1. Order invites calmness. Calmness precedes clear thought. Clear thought makes way for success. You don't have to become an organization fanatic; just devote a little time each day to creating order in your home and office. Pay special attention to important areas. If you're struggling at work, keep your desk more orderly than usual; if you're at odds with your mate, see to it that your bedroom stays neat.

2. Life adds life. Healthy pets, healthy plants, cut flowers still brightly in bloom—these signs of life in a home nourish the people who live there emotionally and spiritually. Views of nature from your windows and paintings of nature on your walls help, too.

3. Heritage brings stability. Remember where you came from. Display photos of your grandparents and great-grandparents. Give your favorite heirlooms a place of honor.

4. The elements grant strength. We're not talking Periodic Table here. It's the ancient elements of water, wood, earth, metal, and fire that should have balanced representation in your environment. According to *feng shui* practitioner Liz Brown, an aquarium contains every element: water, wood (plants), earth (sand), metal (rocks), and fire (as living beings, the fish themselves contain the fire of life).

5. Expansiveness grants abundance. Create a feeling of space in your space. Eliminate furniture and decorations that you don't use or don't love. Choose paint colors that make your rooms look larger, and in tight spaces trick the eye with mirrors. According to *feng shui,* a feeling of spaciousness in the kitchen is especially important for financial well-being.

6. *Movement draws* chi. The movement of wind chimes, music (sound waves), a bubbling fountain, a ceiling fan, a banner, a mobile, or a pendulum clock encourages favorable *chi.*

7. *Light and color in your world put light and color in your life.* Sunlight and full-spectrum bulbs (sold in natural-food stores) lift spirits and outlooks. So do colors that appeal to you. *Feng shui* lore suggests that purple attracts riches, green improves health, and red brings good luck. The rainbow potential of a crystal prism hung where it can catch the sun combines the benefits of both color and light.

8. *Every object has symbolic as well as pragmatic meaning.* Ideally, every item in your house or apartment should have real value, either useful or sentimental, for at least one person in the household. Weed out the superfluous on a regular basis: spring cleaning with a follow-up yard sale is good *feng shui.*

9. *You create your own auspiciousness.* We say that some people make their own luck. To the *feng shui* exponent, this is literal truth. Collaborate with nature. Value beauty. Respect your intuitive inklings about the colors, shapes, textures, and patterns that populate your personal world. Create an environment that entices fortune.

I'll give you a head start by ending these suggestions with number 9. In Chinese tradition, nine represents fullness, success, and abundance.

14.

RETIRE YOUR TOO-TOO

When you cease limiting your possibilities, you can live so that every day brings gifts as welcome as a check in the mail.

As a little girl, I beamed with pride the day I got that pink net emblem of balletic achievement: the tutu. I wore it with youthful glee until that pubescent Saturday morning when I caught a glimpse of myself in the floor-to-ceiling mirror at The Myldred Lyons School of Dance. "Ditch the tutu," I chastised myself, "You're too fat."

What I now realize is that I shed the wrong homonym. The tutu was fine. What needed to go was the *too-too,* that largely but not exclusively female affliction characterized by statements like "I'm *too* heavy," "I'm *too* inexperienced," "I have *too* much baggage," "I have *too* little cash," and "I probably could have done (fill in the blank) but it's *too* late now."

If you have a too-too, give it up. If you have several, clear them out. The only purpose of a too-too is to inflict pain on its possessor. Even the dreary pronouncements I just mentioned would, if the too-too were gone, become starting points for change instead of excuses for misery.

For example: "I'm heavy." Okay. That's a statement of fact. Do you want to accept your body as it is, focus on taking great care of yourself, and enjoy being a voluptuous woman? Or do you want to make the internal and external changes that would make living in a slimmer body realistic and pleasurable? When you delete the "too," the choice is yours.

Or consider: "It's late." Great. You've got incentive. It's not *too* late to learn ballroom dancing, save for a trip to Alaska, or place a singles ad. If you leave out the "too," you can see the reality that, yes, some time has passed since you first had the idea or the yearning, but if you put the necessary process in motion now, you won't lose another minute.

Keep an eye out for your too-toos. They represent a self-defeating thought pattern that's doing you no good. Also be on guard against fitting those around you with too-toos, especially the people who look to you for guidance and affirmation—your employees, your students, or your children.

When you cease limiting your possibilities, you can live so that every day brings gifts as welcome as a check in the mail. A too-too is a major limiter. Look for ways to see yourself and situations that arise without the restrictive "too." This will free you up for discovering alternative routes, gifts in surprising packages, and blessings in disguise.

15.

DO THE NEXT
INDICATED THING

Tending to what needs to be done when it needs doing is
preventive medicine for day-to-day life.

Doing the next indicated thing means taking the next action life presents, whether you're inspired by the prospect or not. The ability to do this is what separates the calm from the crazed. It is a direct route to more time, more peace, and more fulfillment.

The next indicated thing is occasionally momentous, but more often it appears insignificant. It's finishing the filing you started before lunch, getting the mail out of the box, taking off your make-up when you get in late and want to skip it just this once. As pedestrian as all this seems, steering us toward the next indicated thing is an important way life nudges us in the direction we're supposed to be going. If we too often bypass what is at hand and detour onto something else, obligations can become overwhelming and get us off course.

Our various responsibilities can seem like a roomful of unruly kindergartners shouting, "Pick me! Me first!" There are a variety of ways to get them to line up and take their turn. One is to assign an A, B, or C to all the things you think you have to do. A-level tasks are crucial to creating the life you want, personally or professionally; a B goes to what is necessary but not critical; and everything else gets a C.

You can refine this further by numbering the A's 1, 2, and 3, the B's 1, 2, and so forth, according to the importance of each individual action. That way you'll have a straightforward guide to the next indicated thing. If you get through only the A's, you've had a successful day. If you're willing to let some C's fall by the wayside without angst over letting them go, you've had a serene day, too.

Another approach to ascertaining the next indicated thing is to simply be on the lookout for it. It's like putting together a jig-saw puzzle: of all the available pieces, there is really just one that you need to be concerned with now. Trust your inner knowing (see Secret 74, "Trust Your Instincts"). You are the definitive authority on your own life. Listen. What is your next indicated thing to do? A part of you always knows.

Whether you take the rational or the intuitive approach—or combine them to get the best of both worlds—tending to what needs to be done when it needs doing is preventive medicine for day-to-day life. Calling the roofer, when that is the next right thing to do, immediately gives you a sense of peace and order, even if the leak will still be there until the end of the week when he can fit you in.

With all its boons, doing the next indicated thing may not be either thrilling or easy. Eleanor Roosevelt said, "We must do the thing we think we cannot do." The next indicated thing is frequently like that. Have you ever felt that you could climb the Matterhorn more easily than you could do the dishes? That's because the Matterhorn is somewhere else and the dishes are right here. The next indicated thing can seem burdensome because it is so clearly what you're supposed to be doing. It's hard to rationalize away something so obvious.

In doing that thing, however—the thing that may be nagging or difficult—you develop courage. In doing the thing that seems tedious or boring, you develop poise. In doing the thing that looks to be beneath you, or just not what you want to do right now, you develop character. Keep at it and you will generate a presence about yourself that may not have been there before. People will see you as calmer and more efficient, and you will see your life as less hectic and more within your control.

16.

LIVE YOUR LIFE
IN CHAPTERS

*A charmed life is lived in chapters, the way you would read
a long novel . . . . Give yourself without reservation to
the chapter you're on.*

Somehow the notion cropped up that we'd better do everything today. The idea took hold, and now almost everybody believes it. This is why so many women are running nonstop just to keep up. In a frantic attempt to realize their dreams, the dreams retreat and the frantic feeling takes hold.

A charmed life is different, because you live it in chapters, the way you would read a long novel. When you're engrossed in a story, nothing exists except what is happening now. Even though chapter 10 is laying the foundation for chapter 11, the book only makes sense one chapter at a time.

When you live your life this way—focusing on one chapter now, another later—you can devote more unfettered attention to what is yours to do at this time of your life, a time that will never come again. Look at the chapter you're now living. You may be in the college chapter, the crummy-first-job chapter, the home-with-small-kids chapter, or the second-career chapter. Circumstances can certainly make things more complicated and less clear-cut than these examples, but if you can keep in mind the main point of your present life chapter, you can give it priority.

Chapter living is the rational way to "have it all," because when you live this way you're not expecting to have it all at once. Its essence is paying close attention to the current chapter and not worrying about what you may be missing from prior or future ones. Their times are past, or yet to come.

The key is letting go of the compulsion to pursue every possible opportunity right now—even if pursuing it means a crowded life, an alienated family, or a hospital stay for exhaustion. That old saying about opportunity only knocking once is as archaic as the flat-earth theory and as patently untrue. Opportunity knocks all the time—and it rings your doorbell, calls you up, and sends you e-mails.

Ignore the message that keeps repeating "You aren't getting any younger." It's true, of course, in the literal sense, but the unspoken rest of the sentence—"and therefore you'd better do everything now"—is hogwash. Sure, some pursuits need to be taken up early—gymnastics for certain, linguistics maybe—and of course there is a real biological clock that puts a cut-off age on childbearing. Beyond these few specific instances, though, maturity helps, rather than hinders, any dream or aspiration you have.

Believing that everything has to happen in some preset order is another stumbling block to living your life one intriguing chapter at a time. So many people go to school, land a job, get married, buy a house, have kids, work longer, and retire to Florida that we're duped into thinking that this sequence of events is somehow encoded in our DNA. It isn't. If any or all of these particular life experiences are important to you, by all means work toward them—but even then, you don't have to experience them in the expected order.

Instead of going straight to college, I took a low-level clerical job, saved up, and moved to England for a fashion design course. I was dreadful at it, but I parlayed that background into fascinating jobs in fashion and journalism well before I got my B.A. as a married woman of thirty-one. Later, I turned to freelance writing, which enabled me to be at home with my daughter. I thought that this apparent stepping back from the professional world would impede my career, but instead, doors opened that never would have otherwise.

Decide what chapters you want in your life story. Accept that fate may insert a few others. Give yourself without reservation to the chapter you're on. Trust that living this chapter fully will prepare you for what will next unfold. Don't worry that a choice like putting off college to volunteer overseas or taking time from your career to be with your children is foolhardy. Such an experience will make you richer as a person and more valuable to the world. It could also be the finest chapter in your biography.

17.

ENLARGE YOUR WORLD

*Without bags of money or the temperament of a
Marco Polo, we can all enlarge our world.*

My friend Martha has on the wall of her office a world map of
such generous proportions that you always know what country
you're looking at: Botswana, Czech Republic, United Arab
Emirates. This map is perfect for Martha, because she so comfortably inhabits the world at large. She has lived in Germany,
England, India, and Japan, and she's traveled just about everywhere else. Her housemate is a Tibetan monk. Martha needs a
big map because she lives in a big world, one that is colorful,
exciting, and enticing.

For the first time in history, just about anybody can live in a
sphere of this magnitude. Without bags of money or the temperament of a Marco Polo, we can all enlarge our world.

Travel is the most direct way to gain a global perspective. Even
with all there is to learn from reading and talking to people and
watching TV, the other side of the planet can seem fictitious until
you've set foot on it. Not everyone who lives a charmed life has
traveled a lot or even wants to, but if you have the desire to experience personally other places and cultures, look for opportunities
to do it. If the opportunities aren't forthcoming, make some.

Should the prospect of leaving home seem frightening, talk
with travelers in your same situation and find out how they do it.

Single women, parents with children in tow, and low-budget voyagers both young and old are all over the place. Read the travel pages. Just realizing that *somebody* goes to Fiji puts going there yourself in the realm of possibility.

Until you're able to take your grand tour—or the first of several—enlarge your world in other ways:

Read newspapers from other places. Every so often, get a copy of an English language newspaper from somewhere else—the *International Herald-Tribune*, *The London Times*, or *The South China Morning Post.* A different vantage point can make a substantial difference in what the news of the day looks like.

Shop in an exotic market. Even midsized U.S. cities often have Asian, African, European, and Latin American food shops to explore. Treat your kids to coconut candy from Mexico, white caramels from China, or rice paper confections from Japan.

Expose yourself to the arts of the world. Unfamiliar forms of music, dance, painting, and sculpture can expand the parameters of what you consider beautiful and moving. So can foreign films. The universality of human experience comes through poignantly in films from Rumania, Iran, India—everywhere someone has a camera.

Befriend people from other countries. Have them over for dinner. Ask them questions. Stay in touch with some of the people you meet while traveling, even if it's just a card once a year.

Study a language. Once you start, occasions to use what you're learning will crop up.

Learn how other people see things. Different cultures have different religious beliefs, mores, and explanations of how things are and how they should be. In being conversant with these, you don't have to adopt them as your own; simply understand that from where someone else sits, the world looks this way.

Expand your world within as well as without. Scientists learn about the universe through both telescopes and microscopes. There is unfathomable vastness in both directions. We expand our world in the telescopic sense by learning about other people and places. We expand it in the microscopic sense by getting to know ourselves better, investigating our family heritage, and finding out the names of the trees and shrubs in our own garden.

18.

CHANGE WITH
THE SEASONS

The year rotates through the seasons like a wheel of fortune. Being present to each one, possessing its bounty and taking its inconveniences in stride, means living to the fullest every day of the life you get.

The seasons are the moods of the year. Even in locales where seasonal changes are subtle, there are different energies to summer and spring, winter and fall. When we change with the seasons, we put ourselves in harmony with nature. This helps us flow with the current instead of fighting against it.

The times at which the seasons turn are particularly powerful. Ancient people celebrated these as the high points of the year, and the Christian holy days of Christmas and Easter closely approximate the winter solstice and spring equinox.

Make note of the week leading up to and following the twenty-first day of March, June, September, and December. Use that time to contemplate the season that's winding down and the one just unfolding. There's no better time to clean out and pare down. Whether it's cluttered closets, undone tasks, or a backlog of mental paraphernalia that's holding you back, use the energy of the change-of-season time to do something about it.

One change you probably already make as the seasons shift is in your wardrobe. This used to be done even more. Summer meant cotton, winter meant wool, and Memorial Day was when everybody knew to get out their white shoes. With the advent of seasonless fabrics and relaxed rules about what's appropriate, we no longer do a complete changeover. Nevertheless, think as you trade your billowy summer dresses for sweaters and tweeds that you're responding as much to an inner sense of seasonality as to the extended forecast.

It's also good to make a few changes in decor as the year goes through its phases. Something as simple as a season-specific bedspread or comforter can be a pleasant reminder that you're keeping in step with nature's progressions. As you bring plants inside before the first frost, or replace flowered summer china with more substantial stoneware, or bring out the board games no one played from May to September, see these actions less as chores and more as rituals, as ways to be in harmony.

We also make different food choices during different seasons. Be conscious of your pantry's various faces. Even though most foods are now available throughout the year, buying produce in season keeps you in sync with nature's rhythms. Peaches and watermelon; apples and corn; oranges and persimmons; tender lettuce and the first berries—it's like having a calendar you can eat.

Be aware of your cooking patterns and your food cravings. Your stove probably gets used more in fall and winter—the same time you're apt to notice hankerings for soup and chili and hot cereal. In summer, juicy fruits and salads and frozen desserts have appeal. Follow your leanings. Our bodies have retained more of their connection to nature than our minds have. We would do well to trust them more.

There is still, however, a mental and emotional link with the seasons that technology and modernity have not eradicated. We do think, feel, and respond to life differently at different times of the year. If you keep old journals, you can test this assumption by reading what you wrote last January, the preceding July, the following April. You're apt to see a pattern.

In winter, people tend to be their most protective, pensive, and home-centered. In spring, we want to go out into the world and see what's there—like a shoot springing up from the earth. Summer is for being wild, free, and breaking away (thus the summer vacation). Autumn invites us back and quiets us down with nesting, settling in, preparing for winter. Look at your attitude as the seasons cycle. Listen for your quietest inclinations; in the midst of busy days, they can be easy to miss.

Also, respect that you probably have a preferred season or two when you feel your best and do your finest work. I love the fall. I can't remember being sad in October. In late summer, when the heat and humidity I despise are peaking, I remember that fall is on its way and I start to feel that there is something delicious to look forward to. In spring, I make sure that the coming summer, the season I'd just as soon skip, includes plans for something I'll absolutely adore—something indoors or farther north.

The year rotates through the seasons like a wheel of fortune. Being present to each one, possessing its bounty and taking its inconveniences in stride, means living to the fullest every day of the life you get.

19.

FACTOR IN DOWN TIME

Develop a higher opinion of free time, transition time, or even (I know this is tough) doing nothing.

None of us spends every minute being productive, happy, charming, giving, industrious, and on top of things. Whole days can seem to count for nothing. Don't worry about it. It's the way things work.

I've always been fascinated by sleep. The body of every animal is able to repair itself only when its inhabitant is, for all intents and purposes, gone. Some people resent the time they spend sleeping and jeopardize their well-being by cutting back. Similarly, lots of us feel indignant about down time, especially when an entire day goes by and we think there is nothing concrete to show for it.

If you are using the principles in this book—and simply by being the sort of person who would read this book—you already have fewer days than most people that seem to be swallowed by black holes. Another way to cut their number is to accept the ones you get. Allow for down time, even twenty-four hours' worth. Your body needs sleep for repair and healing; likewise, your life needs down time so you can regroup, reassess, and go forward.

Accede to this fact of life more easily by doing the nightly exercise of examining your day from bottom to top. As you lie in bed tonight, think back from that moment through your various activities all the way back to the time you awoke this morning. As you scan your day, you'll see that it was not wasted. You paid someone an honest compliment. You watched a movie that made you laugh. You put gas in your car. If you come across something you're unhappy with—like an angry outburst or some sloppy work—make a mental note to do something tomorrow to redeem the situation. In this way, you've already guaranteed that tomorrow will not be a waste either, and it isn't even here yet.

This works for coming to grips not only with unproductive days but with those that are downright unpleasant—the ones whose only redeeming feature is that at midnight they'll end. Finding the snatches of good that did make their way into a really bad day can be a godsend.

Something else that can help is to appreciate that every day has some time that's unaccounted for. If you've ever tried to work one of those time-management systems that asks you to write down what you do every minute of the day, you know how frustrating it can be. You might write, "10:00 to 10:25—ironing," but you know that in addition to ironing you took two phone calls, petted the cat, and got on the floor for the anti-backache exercise you almost always have to do when you iron.

Real life defies being filed in tight compartments. We all need down time—playing a game of solitaire on the computer, chatting at the water cooler, reading the parts of the paper that don't fall under "keeping informed." Develop a higher opinion of free time, transition time, or even (I know this is tough) doing nothing. For men, doing nothing is almost a sacrament. We can learn from them to think better of it.

I see this often as a writer. My work ethic tells me that I have to put in four hours at my desk *writing*. No letters. No straightening up. No phone calls, even for business. *Writing*. (Some people have an inner child, others an inner sergeant.) If I blindly follow these orders without preliminary down time, I end up staring at a blank screen. If instead I putter some before my workday starts—do my nails, pay some bills, expound at length in my journal, or go out for breakfast—ideas come to me that beg to get on paper. That way, when I do write, I actually have something to say.

A lot of women believe that they can't have discretionary down time because their lives are too full. The problem with this is that down time, like sleep, is going to come after you if you don't go after it. Give yourself breaks—even five-minute ones—throughout the day and watch your efficiency increase. This is because you'll more often be inviting down time in and less often having it show up unannounced. You'll be in control—even when you're only looking out the window.

20.

COMPLICATE
SELECTIVELY

*Lives that work tend to issue from a blend of simplicity
and selective complication. Let's face it: our greatest joys
complicate our lives the most.*

Simplicity is what you get when you remove from your life certain complications: items that don't serve or delight you, and activities that take more energy than they give back. Even before simplicity became a movement, it was a good idea. It's appealing, too, because it lends itself to quick fixes and pithy counsel: "Every time you bring something new into your house, get rid of something." "Touch every piece of mail only once." "If you haven't used it in a year, pass it on."

In studying this topic at length, and in assiduously working to keep my own affairs reasonably simple, I have come to think that the matter is not so cut-and-dried. Lives that work tend to issue from a blend of simplicity and *selective complication*. Let's face it: our greatest joys complicate our lives the most. Travel, for instance, is a terrific disruption requiring shopping, spending, packing, passports, time off work, hiring a house sitter, putting a hold on the mail, suffering jet lag, and maybe two months on malaria pills.

Relationships are worse. Before I married William, I fancied myself a doyenne of simple living. It took only an "I do" to legally bind me to a four-story house, a microwave oven, and cable TV. Of course, William married into my complexities too. He took on my unpredictable schedule on the lecture circuit, three cats, and a dog who carries being man's best friend to a licking and wagging extreme. The complications that leach serenity from a life, however, are those that don't offer sufficient compensation. William and I give each other deeper joy than can be diminished by the fact that he came into the marriage with a channel-clicker and I with an affectionate menagerie.

When you do seek to simplify, either singly or in tandem, you need to know yourself better than at any other time. This is because the process asks you to discard objects, activities, and habits you may have had so long that they seem like another limb. You want to be sure in any scaling-down effort that you're disposing of what you yourself know to be extraneous. For example, I read somewhere that it simplifies your life to get rid of your cell phone. Funny, but that particular accoutrement of our era has simplified my life no end. I no longer worry about getting lost or stranded, and the security benefits mean even more now that my daughter is about to drive.

Just as I disagree with the no-cell-phone expert, however, some people disagree with me. In presentations I give outlining simplicity strategies, I always start with my favorite: paying for purchases in cash (see Secret 41, "Prosper"). This keeps my finances clean, aboveboard, and simple. It makes it impossible to spend money I don't have. I love it. But more than once someone has come up to me after a talk and said, "We use our charge card for everything—groceries, gas, eating out. That way, other than the mortgage and utilities, we only have to write one check a month. It's so simple." Simplicity, like beauty, is highly subjective.

In general, simplifying means letting go of certain beliefs that we hold onto more tenaciously than that dress we keep thinking will come back in style. We might believe, for instance, that we have to answer the telephone just because it is ringing. Or that shopping for its own sake is legitimate recreation. Or that we can part with certain items only if someone pays us a good price for them, instead of comprehending that sometimes the profit is in just knowing they're gone.

In the end, we do what we think will make us happy. Sometimes a move we make in the direction of happiness only makes a muddle of things. That's when we need to simplify in short order before we get to the point of thinking we can never dig out. At other times, though, we consciously take on a complicated situation—taking in a foster child perhaps, or bringing an elderly parent to live with us—and know, even during the most trying times, that this is the best decision we ever made.

This is the essence of selective complication: paring down the possessions and occupations that rob you of hours and energy so you're free to focus on what matters to you. Then if there's clutter, it's the residue of projects you're passionate about. If there are complications, you'll have chosen them instead of the other way around.

21.

DRINK GOOD COFFEE,
EAT GOOD FOOD

*Make it a point to eat a minimum of one meal a day sitting
at a table and using utensils. Flowers, candles, cloth
napkins, and dishes that would break if you dropped them
are extra credit.*

A chalkboard at my favorite café admonishes "Drink good coffee, eat good food." I never noticed it until the night of the concert. Another customer, a man in his forties, I'd say, put his cup on top of the upright piano that I'd thought was there just for decoration, or because it was too heavy to move out. He then sat down and started to play—movie themes, Gershwin, Broadway scores, light classics. I was serenaded for an hour for the price of a *latté* and *panini*.

As he played I realized that I was immersed in quality—good coffee, good food, good music—and I grieved just a little over all the times I'd settled for less. People who live well drink good coffee—or tea or juice or water or wine. They eat good food: delicious, healthful, and nicely presented. They wear good clothes—not necessarily expensive but comfortable, becoming, and well-maintained. They treat themselves to uplifting films and plays and performances. The subject matter might be somber, even tragic, but the quality of the work can move the spirit just the same.

Living well could stand to be more widely practiced. For example, everybody eats, but few people dine. This is such a loss. And because we're in the final sputters of decades of dieting obsession, we have the opportunity to fabricate a new, liberating definition of "good food" for our daughters and sons. Good food is real—that is, it grew, or its primary ingredients grew. It is edible without benefit of chemistry. Eating good food, like reading good books, is worth sitting down for. It's worth sharing with people you care about or, if you are eating alone, good food is worth savoring—without watching TV, and certainly not while driving a car.

Eating on the run has increased in direct proportion to our *being* on the run. Some activities are consequential enough that anyone who wants an intensely pleasurable stay on earth simply must make time for them. Meals are one of these. Make it a point to eat a minimum of one meal a day sitting at a table and using utensils. Flowers, candles, cloth napkins, and dishes that would break if you dropped them are extra credit.

Even when you are in a hurry, add a little quality to the experience every time you eat or drink. It takes no more time to pour your morning juice or smoothie into a stemmed goblet than into a plastic tumbler with superheroes on it. (I realize that quality is relative: James and Erik, my young stepsons, would find more of it with the superheroes.)

If you are in such a rush that you absolutely cannot eat something resembling quality food in a quality environment, I offer a radical suggestion: don't eat. Unless you have a medical condition that requires eating on a strict schedule, waiting won't hurt you. When I was in college, Dr. Jeremiah Cameron, English professor, was once incensed that several of us were munching candy bars during his lecture on *Macbeth*. "This is preposterous," he roared. "You ought to fast for your souls."

It seemed at the time a rather drastic declaration, but in twenty-five years I haven't forgotten it. I also don't eat candy bars anymore. If I want chocolate, I have the good stuff: rich and dark and carved into a wonderful little sculpture of a heart or a flower or a gold brick.

Start with what goes into your mouth, and go from there to elevate the quality of the "food" you put into your mind and heart. Some books and movies and discussions are like a meal prepared with skill and served with love. Others are the mental equivalent of pork rinds and powdered drink mix.

Tuck away for yourself the snippet of sagacity: "Drink good coffee, eat good food." Apply it to every habit, purchase, and pastime meant to nourish you physically or spiritually. *Bon appétit.*

22.

RAZZLE-DAZZLE
ON OCCASION

You are already in possession of the seven components of
substantive razzle-dazzle. Use them properly and
you will radiate star quality.

There is work to be done. There are commitments to keep. Just maintaining a body, soul, house, family, and whatever else you've got going takes energy and focus. To live a charmed life, however, it is appropriate sometimes—necessary, in fact—to go for some razzle-dazzle.

Razzle-dazzle is a vaudevillian term originally applied to the bells, whistles, and special effects that would elicit from an audience oohs, ahs, and repeat ticket sales. When you pull out the stops and go for a bit of razzle-dazzle in your life, you're using a similar tactic. Today we're at no loss for glitz, but razzle-dazzle with substance to shore it up is as hard to come by as it was in Flo Ziegfeld's day.

Nevertheless, you are already in possession of the seven components of substantive razzle-dazzle. Use them properly and you will radiate star quality. An invisible red carpet will roll out before you wherever you go.

1. Razzle-dazzle with talent. If you can sing, you already razzle-dazzle me because I can't carry a tune. I am similarly awestruck if you have ever passed a swimming test, or if you can draw anything recognizable, do math beyond basic algebra, or keep an African violet alive. To people who cannot do what you can—most people can't, you know—your talents are dazzling. Develop them. Express them. Get comfortable wowing your fellow humans.

2. Razzle-dazzle with readiness. You may have heard the tired joke "My ship came in but I was waiting at the airport." Plenty of people miss opportunities because they're in the wrong place, or they're late, or they're just not ready. Be ready. Learn what you need to know and meet the people you need to know. Keep your affairs in order so you don't have to pass on chances to soar because of some personal entanglement. And put yourself together every time you leave the house. You may not be discovered at a soda fountain like a classic movie star, but you never know who you'll run into.

3. Razzle-dazzle with quality. Rarity dictates value. We live in an era of excess; quantity no longer guarantees razzle-dazzling. Quality, always at a premium, is another matter. Infuse your life with it. Acquire fewer possessions and let the ones you have epitomize beauty or usefulness. Do quality work, whether typing a letter or teaching a child. Live a quality life through the good you do and the dignity you maintain.

4. Razzle-dazzle with "Yes!" Caution is called for when walking alone at night or when camping near bears. Otherwise, hesitancy is overrated. If an offer, an option, or an opportunity strikes a chord with your deepest self, just say yes. Figure out the logistics later if you have to. Scary? Sure. That's why it will razzle-dazzle everybody who's still cogitating, contemplating, and mumbling something like "I'll have to get back to you on that."

5. *Razzle-dazzle with freedom.* Nothing is as attractive or desirable to the human spirit as freedom. If yours is lacking in any area, do something about it. If you have an addiction, go for recovery. If you have a debt, pay it. If lack of education keeps you tied to a job or a life that limits who you are, go back to school. Do whatever it takes for you to be free. The enslaved will be amazed. You might even inspire some of them to break free, too.

6. *Razzle-dazzle by bouncing back.* When the magician's assistant who was chopped in half emerges unscathed, the audience applauds this hefty dose of razzle-dazzle. The world responds similarly when any of us bounces back after things go wrong. It's easier to succumb to adversity than win over it. When you do come out on the other side of a difficulty—shaken maybe, but still standing—you enter the charmed circle of the triumphant.

7. *Razzle-dazzle with follow-through.* There is always a crowd at the starting line; those who stay with a project, make good on a promise, and finish what they start comprise a far smaller group. Join them if you haven't already. Keep on through the hard parts. Meet your deadlines. Do a little extra. Muster as much enthusiasm for the end as for the beginning.

Although knowing how to razzle-dazzle will open doors for you that would otherwise stay shut, its value lies as much in inspiring yourself as in impressing others. Give 'em a little razzle-dazzle. You may not stop the show every night, but you'll always have a part.

23.

AGE EXQUISITELY

*The ultimate secret to aging exquisitely is to
identify more with the part of yourself that
doesn't grow older—the inner part—and less
with the outer part that metamorphoses
through ages and stages all your life long.*

Our spiritual selves get more beautiful as the years pass. Unfortunately, spiritual beauty doesn't usually get on the cover of *Cosmo*. Because we live in a culture that doesn't know what to do with women who have attained wisdom, we can fear reaching that state ourselves. This means that in addition to dashing through the day to beat the clock, a lot of women dash through their lives to beat the calendar, hounded by a sense that they'd better hurry up because there isn't much time.

The fact is, there is more time for us than there has ever been. Women today start new careers at fifty and take up new sports at seventy. In spite of the evidence of this at any tennis court, too many of us still feel pressure to get things done right away, before we pass our prime. This flies in the face of the real truth: that we decide when our prime hits and how long it lasts.

Everything we do today is creating our future. In one way, we spend our youth designing our old age. Choose to live an exquisite life all your life by putting into place the physical, mental, and spiritual disciplines that offer the best odds for happiness in the future.

Make a plan. Decide this minute that your golden years really will be golden—whether you're sixteen or sixty when you read this. Visualize the way you want to be at seventy, eighty, ninety. And put into practice *now* the actions that will most likely result in the life you want *then.*

Take care of your body as if it had to last a lifetime. Protect yourself from the sun—not just beach sun, lunch-hour sun, too. Stay limber as well as fit: take up yoga, or at least sit on the floor often enough that you never forget how. Eat better than you did yesterday and take a multi-vitamin-and-mineral supplement. Drink lots of water; it may not be the fountain of youth, but it is the difference between a plum and a prune.

Take risks. A large survey asked seniors what they would change if they could do things over. The majority responded that, although they would have taken better care of their health, they would have taken more risks in their lives. They cited both physical risks, like skydiving and hang gliding, and emotional risks—expressing their feelings and letting themselves be more vulnerable to the people closest to them.

Have role models. Follow the lead of women you admire who have exquisitely achieved advanced age. Talk with those you can and read about the others. Let them be your teachers and guides. I have several. One is Gloria Swanson: I love the stories of her carrying special health foods and bottled water wherever she went. A role model I actually know is my own mother. She gave herself a computer and Internet hookup for her eighty-first birthday—and she helped out with this chapter.

Get to know your spiritual self. When a woman plugs into her divine nature, astounding events transpire. First, she realizes that she is not an aging physical body that might have a soul somewhere. Instead, she is a timeless soul inhabiting a body. With this realization, growing older becomes less threatening. Moreover, women with active inner lives stay physically and mentally younger. They worry less about getting older, and it seems to happen more slowly. The ultimate secret to aging exquisitely is to identify more with the part of yourself that doesn't grow older— the inner part—and less with the outer part that metamorphoses through ages and stages all your life long.

As you make your plans and goals and resolutions, realize that you're laying the foundation for what is to come. You have the power to eliminate many regrets before they materialize. You can live to have silver hair and great-great-grandchildren without ever feeling old.

24.

STOP TO REALIZE

*Make a practice of stopping every so often to simply be
present to the present: what you see, what you smell,
who is with you, how this moment feels physically
and emotionally.*

It's fun to watch people with camcorders. They document everything in sight and make pronouncements like, "These are the stairs." We would do well to notate our lives with such thoroughness. Actually, we do this every time we stop to realize what we're experiencing. In taking a moment to step back from our lives and observe them, we can assimilate a bit of beauty, a slice of synchronicity, or a stroke of luck. Stopping to notice these encourages their repeat visits.

We lose a lot of life by simply not letting it in. Someone tells us something and we say, "Uh-huh" without really paying attention. Or we take something wonderful for granted ("So it's a beautiful day. What do you expect in San Diego?"). Or we're doing so many things at once that none of them gets our full attention.

One way our minds look out for us is through a switch-off mechanism that can kick in during times of extreme physical pain or acute emotional trauma. Because we are so busy nowadays, this protective device sometimes shows up during perfectly pleasant episodes. We subject ourselves to so many stimuli that our internal gatekeeper seeks to shield us from the excess by arbitrarily select-ing events to register only partially. If we do not remind ourselves to really take in a particular sensation or encounter, we can go through the motions without allowing an experience to imprint and enrich us.

If you make a practice of stopping every so often simply to be present to the present—what you see, what you smell, who is with you, how this moment feels physically and emotionally—you are well on your way to getting the maximum amount of life out of your life. Another technique for maximizing peak experiences is to take a few minutes as soon as possible after an event to ade-quately take in what went on.

Some time back, I was visiting New York and sat at a lecture next to a woman named Lea. Afterward, we walked together for a few blocks and I learned that Lea, just like me, writes and regu-larly practices yoga. We made a lunch date. After she went her way, I just stopped. It was only for a minute there on the corner of Fifty-second Street and Park Avenue, but I stopped in the midst of the crowd and the noise and the hubbub to fully absorb the fact that, far from home, I had just met a stranger who would become a friend. I couldn't just let that pass, hail a taxi, and go on to the next thing without pausing to let this impromptu gift of grace sink in.

This practice of stopping is especially important during major turning points—reunions, rites of passage, special trips. These are events we want to experience thoroughly but that we risk losing because they so often take place when the life around them is going at a fever pitch. When William and I got married, we borrowed from the Jewish tradition a wedding custom that allows the bride and groom fifteen minutes alone immediately following the ceremony. What precious time this was! Plans, preparations, houseguests, and hoopla had taken most of our energy for days before. The ceremony had been beautiful, but public. In the quarter-hour following it, though, we were able to touch base with each other and remember the reason for all the ado.

If the prospect of stopping is intimidating because you think you might miss something, remember that without stopping, you could miss everything. Look for places in your experience where a pause can be inserted. Saying grace or sitting in silence for a few moments before meals is such an insertion. Setting aside time to regroup when you get home from work or from a day out is another. So is slipping into a quiet room for some intentional breathing (see Secret 26, "Breathe") when you're feeling tense or angry. In the midst of whatever is happening, take a realization break every so often. Then, when you're on the go again, you'll go further.

25.

OBEY THE LAWS

The Laws I'm talking about comprise ageless wisdom that
shows up in every culture. This is the big stuff,
yet each Law is directly and practically applicable
in any purposeful life.

Break the rules all you want, but obey the Laws. The rules are the various customs and mores that people come up with to make sense of things and maintain a comfortable status quo. Rules vary depending upon where you are and whom you ask. You can recognize rules because they often include the words *should* or *shouldn't*. Examples are "You shouldn't make more money than your husband"; "You shouldn't major in art history because computer science is where the jobs are"; "You should have short hair after you're forty" (or thirty or twenty-five).

There are thousands of rules, many of which we'd be better off without. Laws, on the other hand, are few but imperative. I'm not referring here to the laws enacted by governing bodies. Some of these reflect actual Laws; others are just rules that got a promotion. You obey these laws because you're a citizen of wherever you live. The Laws I'm talking about, however, are the Laws of Life. They're universal and comprise what Aldous Huxley called the "Perennial Philosophy," ageless wisdom that shows up in every culture. This is the big stuff, yet each Law is directly and practically applicable in any purposeful life.

You're heard these Laws before. Unfortunately, they can get mixed up with rules and be tossed aside like the proverbial baby with the bathwater. Use your discernment. Extract the essential from the extraneous. These Laws are not secret or esoteric. In addition to appearing in every major religion, they are as plain as day to anybody who observes the way things work.

These are the Laws that are most obvious to me. Any others you need you either know already or you'll figure out now that you have them on your mind:

What you do comes back to you. From this comes "Do unto others as you would have them do unto you." It's called The Golden Rule, but it's really a Law. It means that we're not powerless pawns who have no say in our destiny, but that instead we get back in kind what we put out.

No action is lost. This means that all the hard stuff—effort, discipline, getting up for work some winter Monday when it's not light yet—is worth doing. It also means that nothing we do is insignificant, and that even a seemingly small act can have a wide ripple effect.

Few events are random. Life is more purposeful than we think in our day-to-day living of it. This is easiest to understand when you look back on past incidents and see how one led to another. More than chance is operative.

Thoughts create circumstances. The greatest strength we have is the ability to shape our thoughts to help bring about the life we want. Our thoughts are templates we extend into the future, where we can fill them in and actualize them. Positive thinking isn't a game. It's more like laying a foundation.

Hate destroys the one who has it. Forgiveness isn't always easy, tolerance can be a chore, and there is a certain satisfaction in the conviction that "we" are the good guys and "they" have no redeeming features. Nevertheless, the Law remains. Even "righteous indignation" can be hostility parading as virtue—Dante called it the first level of hell.

We're all connected. We are inextricably connected to all people, all life, all nature, and all that is. Our astonishing uniqueness and individuality notwithstanding, we're cells in a larger body. We need to live with the understanding that what we do affects the entire organism. Francis Thompson saw this connection when he wrote, "Thou canst not disturb a flower without troubling a star."

Happiness comes from inside. Most people start looking for happiness through what they can get and eventually realize that it comes instead from what they are. It is more effective to choose to be happy today than to wait for outer circumstances to make us that way.

Love is the main thing. This can be confusing because we think of love primarily as an emotion. We "fall in love" or we say, "I love your dress." But there's much more to it. As the officiant at a wedding I once attended said, "We are here today to talk about love. Love is not an emotion, because God is love and God is not an emotion." We learn to love by showing love. This is not the same as feeling love. We can show it whether we feel it or not. Show it often enough, and you're likely to feel it too.

26.

BREATHE

Tell yourself as you inhale that you're breathing in life and strength and glorious possibilities. When you exhale, know that you're expelling the mental pressures, aggravations, and limitations that may have held you back.

The little boy in the airport waiting area was distraught—and using all his lung capacity to show it. Dad and Grandma tried in vain to quiet him with toys and promises. When Mom arrived on the scene, she knelt in front of her agitated offspring, looked him in the eye, and said, "David: Breathe." Almost instantaneously the crying turned to quiet, and within minutes, David was scampering about playing and laughing, apparently oblivious to his earlier upset.

Sometimes as adults we need the same message David got: "Breathe." Therapists define anxiety as "physical responses to given stimuli"; the foremost anxiety response is shallow breathing. The ability to breathe slowly and fully counters systematic tenseness and *automatically* replaces it with relaxation.

Regular practice of controlled breathing, even for just a couple of minutes a day, makes a substantial deposit into your serenity account. The same techniques can also be a godsend in situations so stressful that "trying to relax" is an oxymoron—and no more effective than offering a trinket to a howling toddler. Breath control is the ultimate stress manager because it's free, immediate, and always available.

The yogis of ancient India made a science of studying the breath. They taught that oxygen is our primary food and that proper breathing placates the mind—a conclusion with which contemporary psychology concurs. In addition, the yogis believed that the breath not only sustains life but also sustains our moment-to-moment contact with the divine.

Even though breathing is the most basic and constant activity of life, most people are never taught to do it effectively—or they're taught backward. Did you ever hear a gym teacher or fitness instructor say something like, "Take a deep breath and suck in your stomach?" That's absurd. It's like blowing up a balloon to make it smaller. When you inhale, your abdomen is supposed to expand because you're taking in air. You can still "suck in your stomach," but do it on the exhalation.

To breathe like a yogi, sit comfortably, either in a chair with your feet on the floor, or on a mat or a pillow, cross-legged. Keep your back reasonably straight. Think of breathing as a three-part process: you'll expand your abdomen first, then your diaphragm, and finally your chest. This way you'll be sure to fill your lungs instead of settling for the all-too-common superficial breathing that doesn't fully oxygenate the system.

For basic deep breathing, inhale and exhale through your nose. Go at your own pace, remembering to expand your abdomen, diaphragm, and chest in order. Then exhale just as fully, being sure to push out all the stale air when you do. Take it easy. Don't hyperventilate. Discover a comfortable rhythm for yourself. Do this for a minute or two, or for five or six complete breaths. It's a good way to wake up, especially if you do it outside or near an open window. Slow, steady breathing is also a traditional prelude to and accompaniment for meditation. Combining the two multiplies the benefits of both.

In any context, let your thinking enhance your breathing. Tell yourself as you inhale that you're breathing in life and strength and glorious possibilities. When you exhale, know that you're expelling both physical impurities and the mental pressures, aggravations, and limitations that may have held you back.

Use your breath to help you clear your mind, calm your thoughts, and open yourself to inspiration (that word literally means "to breathe in the spirit"). Do some conscious breathing before you take a test—and when you come to an especially tough question. Breathe before the interview. Breathe when you want to bite somebody's head off but know you'd be the one to get indigestion. Proper breathing, say the yogis, can change the pattern of your thoughts. And this, says just about everyone who has looked into the matter, can change the pattern of your life.

27.

DESIGNATE A
LITTLE SACRED SPOT

A little sacred spot is a gift we give ourselves, our homes, and our families—even if they wonder what on earth this is about.

When I was in my early twenties and living in a studio apartment, I read that it was good to have a special room for spiritual practice. It was supposed to exude peace and calm, be clear of distractions, and be enhanced with reminders of what its users consider sacred. "This room," one writer suggested, "should be dedicated to emptiness." I thought at the time, "Good heavens, I don't have enough room for a bed, much less a room for emptiness."

Nevertheless, I cleared a little corner of the space I did have and erected a makeshift altar from a fruit crate, a tie-died sarong (it was the seventies), a votive candle, and dog-eared copies of *The Prophet* and *The Book of Common Prayer*. From that day on, no place I've lived in has been without a spot earmarked for interior exploration.

There are dual benefits to having such a space. First, its very existence encourages practice that could otherwise be overlooked in favor of the world's more pressing requests or more glittering invitations. Second, when you dedicate a corner or a closet, a room or a portion of one, to your spiritual life, its blessings spill over into your life as a whole.

You get this spot by staking claim the way homesteaders did

in the Old West. You have to believe that having this space is more important than whatever you moved out or set aside to get it. If you live with people who don't understand that your soul needs a speck of real estate all its own, stand your ground. Survey the place where you live and attempt to discover areas that feel as if they were waiting to be decreed your sacred spot. Walk slowly through your house or apartment and get a feel for it, as if you were visiting for the first time.

Combine what you learn from your intuitive tour with a pragmatic nod to aesthetics and space available as you locate this site where your inner self can feel particularly at home. When you have it, put a lamp and a chair there, or an altar and a cushion, or leave it as a square yard of Zen-inspired blankness. You'll know what to do.

Use this spot for your morning quiet (see Secret 5, "Take Ten"), to wind down after a busy day, or for thinking through a dilemma. Even when you're not at home, you can visualize this friendly place, close your eyes, and pretend that you're there. Sacred space is portable.

A little sacred spot is a gift we give ourselves, our homes, and our families—even if they wonder what on earth this is about. Sometimes a small reminder of heaven can influence even the solidly down-to-earth. When we moved to the house we now live in, I wondered why we were short on telephone books. It seems that my daughter Rachael, then fourteen, had appropriated a matched set of Yellow Pages, covered them with her old crib quilt and employed them as the foundation for a miniature altar. I gave myself a few minutes to feel elated. Then I ordered more phone books.

28.

PUT UP WITH
SOME DISCOMFORT

*Face discomfort, greet it, and go with it until it matures
into accomplishment, satisfaction, and pride.*

Behind the glory nearly everyone wants to attain is a degree of
discomfort nearly everyone wants to avoid. The ballet that looks
effortless got that way through prior effort. The music we love to
hear was seldom written because a composer heard it in his head
and took dictation. Agony almost always precedes ecstasy. Any
woman who's ever given birth knows that.

Nothing that other people admire got there by accident,
whether it's a clean house, a healthy garden, a prosperous retirement, or a courteous child. It takes grit to study late into the
night or get up before the sun to work out at the gym.

This means calling into our lives what most people assiduously circumvent: discipline, perseverance, regimen, repetition,
and delayed gratification. Think of it as military school for a
charmed life.

This is not to say that discomfort is desirable for its own sake.
But oftentimes, if you're willing to go through just a little of it, it
turns into something else. You've probably experienced, for
example, dreading to exercise but getting started anyway and
feeling great by the time you finish. Similarly, tackling a stack of

correspondence or a pile of wrinkled clothes can look like a summons to misery. But here again, once you're writing or you've got the ironing going, the work takes on a life of its own and can be surprisingly pleasant.

Whether it's the minor discomforts of daily life or some more substantial test of your mettle, you have resources to help you through. Remember that nothing lasts forever; put up with some discomfort now, and forge ahead in spite of it. Believe in what you're doing. And know most of all that you don't go through anything alone.

Come to terms with discomfort by regarding it as part of the price of admission to the life you want. Face discomfort, greet it, and go with it until it matures into accomplishment, satisfaction, and pride. Identify with the discomfort as little as possible so you don't get stuck there. Resist the temptation to converse at length about how excruciating it was to write your dissertation or put down cigarettes. You did it. The people who need to know do know—yourself most of all.

29.

DRAW FROM THE PAST

There is a part of every human being that needs to interact with things that have been around awhile.

In college I did a research paper about the Amish. I read then that an interviewer had asked an Amish farmer why he was against progress. "I'm not against it," he replied. "I just don't want to take it so fast."

There is wisdom in his words for the rest of us. Even if we elect to partake of all the progress we can get our hands on, much comfort can be found in that which has some history, in items and activities that have proven their worth and usefulness.

We see more change in a year than was, not long ago, expected in a lifetime. On the one hand, we're privileged to be around for all the excitement, but on the other, there is a part of every human being that needs to interact with things that have been around awhile. There is consolation in knowing that certain things do persist over time with relatively minor modifications.

One uncomplicated way to draw from the past is with objects: either those that are actually old, or a new rendition of some classic commodity. You needn't become an antique buff to do this. Even if your tastes tend toward the starkly futuristic, you can draw from the past by simply including some representation of the timeless along with the technological.

You might do this by keeping a fountain pen on your desk,

one that is perfectly weighted and shaped to fit your grip. Nice stationery works, too—engraved or embossed or textured with linen in it. For panache, add a letter opener, vintage or not. My friend Suzanne even has a rotary phone. Its benefit to her is not solely aesthetic: when she doesn't use a touch-tone phone, she actually gets to speak to a voice with a human attached instead of the disembodied postmistress of a euphemistic "mailbox."

Your sensibilities to time-honored objects can have a jubilee in the kitchen. Coexisting with the blender and the food processor—which are useful, I don't deny—you might find a sturdy walnut chopping board, springform pans like your mother used for your childhood birthday cakes, and the dishes painted with morning glories that you inherited from your great-aunt. Display some of these where you can see them. Note, too, crossover items like the bread machine, a recent invention that may put the smell of fresh-baked bread into the sense memory of a new generation. And don't underestimate the merits of the comfort foods you remember from childhood, even if you make a somewhat healthier version of them now than you used to.

All over your house and all through your life, look for ordinary things that give you the safe feeling of constancy: rosewater and glycerin hand lotion maybe, or a quilt (my husband's ninety-one-year-old grandmother made ours), or a cotton handkerchief. The response you get from other people to pulling an embroidered hanky from your purse can be staggering. Even those who weren't alive before tissues (that's pretty much everybody) are taken aback by this tiny thing. Expect to be complimented and copied.

Enjoying diversions that have been around for some years is another way to draw from the past. Some people are passionate about this, so they learn to spin or weave or play the lute. For most of us, it's enough to do something as simple as sitting by the fire, reading, telling stories, or playing chess. You can also get a sense of connection to yesterday from going on a picnic, taking a stroll, or having a face-to-face conversation over tea that was brewed or lemonade with lemons in it.

Lost arts are those that people stop sharing with their children. Be sure the ones that typify your heritage and your essence are passed down and passed around.

30.

WATCH YOUR WORDS

*Words form the bridge between mind and matter;
they play a vital role in shaping our reality.*

The words we speak are creative as well as communicative. In
their creative capacity, words form the bridge between mind and
matter; they play a vital role in shaping our reality. If more people
knew this, we would seldom hear laments like, "I'm such a slob,"
"Just my luck," or "I couldn't learn that in a million years." For
someone to say, "This is driving me crazy," or "I could just kill
him!" would be rare and shocking.

Of course we don't mean it when we make these offhand
comments, but our unconscious doesn't know that. People
respond dramatically to a hypnotist's suggestions that their
unconscious perceives as real. Because we give ourselves equally
persuasive suggestions with our own words, we would do well to
avoid the following components of verbal self-sabotage:

Untruths: Most of us don't make a practice of lying, but the
absolute honesty that is transformative and healing is scarce. I'm
not talking about the pettiness and cruelty that can pass for honesty ("I have to be honest with you: That dress is really awful").
Rather, the honesty that is fundamental to a charmed life comes
from courage and character. It can manifest in an act like leaving
a note with your name and phone number on the windshield if
you scratch a car in a parking lot. It also takes the form of the

honesty of coming clean with yourself, admitting a weakness or a problem so you can take steps to eliminate it.

Exaggeration: Exaggeration is the most common way honest people lie. "My company grossed three million dollars last year" (2.2 does not round up to 3). "My grandson has been all over Europe" (Paris and Brussels are not "all over"). Truth without ornamentation emanates clarity and integrity for itself and the one who speaks it.

Absolutes and superlatives: "Everybody hates me." "I can't do anything right." "The whole world has gone to hell in a hand basket." That just about wraps it up, doesn't it? When you use absolutes and superlatives (like "everything," "all the time," "never," and "perfect"), there is very little left to say. You've told your mind that this is a closed case and that you're devoid of further recourse. Besides, absolutes and superlatives are seldom true. There is almost no subject that everybody agrees on and few human activities can be characterized by *never* or *always.*

Self-put-downs: These may start with the desire to be humble, but incessant denial of ourselves, our abilities, and our accomplishments can become a self-fulfilling prophecy. If you say "I'm a real idiot," some dear soul will probably jump in with, "No you're not," but your unconscious puts more stock in your voice than an outsider's. Keep on top of what you say about yourself. You don't have to brag. Just speak of yourself as considerately as you would of someone else.

Diminishment: "Oh, it was nothing" and "I'm not really that good" are noxious sentiments. Say "Thank you" to compliments and let it go at that. Listen on the phone and to answering machine messages for ways people diminish themselves: "I'm just the cleaning lady." "It's only Mom." Avoid this use of "just" and "only," and look out for "but," as in "He's a good baby, but he doesn't sleep through the night," or "I got the job, but the last person who had it couldn't handle it and quit." Speaking well of the good in your life will not scare it away.

Aimless criticism: This is a put-down directed at another person and usually couched so as to sound like help. If you feel compelled to criticize, wait. Give it forty-eight hours. By then you'll know if your desire is to be of use or to say your piece. There are few circumstances in which criticism is genuinely constructive, for the simple reason that most of the time people already see their shortcomings—usually enlarged, enhanced, and in glorious living color. When you must point out a liability, focus as much as you can on the person's assets.

The chameleon complex: Chameleons change color for protection. People can, too, but it's more becoming to lizards. When we want to fit in, it's tempting to alter our opinions to reflect those of the people we're around, and to speak words that don't match our lives. Be who you are wherever you are. Exercise diplomacy where called for and kindness in every circumstance, but don't alter your essence for anybody. The admiration most worth having often comes from someone who disagrees with what you think but respects who you are.

31.

ASK FOR WHAT YOU WANT

*Ask for what you want. You'll be amazed at
how often you get a positive response.*

Because human beings are interdependent, it is virtually impossible to have the life you want without asking other people for
help. When you ask for what you want, the answer is sometimes
no. If you don't ask, the answer is always no.

Women are infamous for failing to ask for what we want.
Many of us learned that hinting and insinuating are the proper
feminine communication techniques. Men get frustrated when
we expect them to be the Psychic Hotline and know what we
want without our having to actually say it. It's exasperating for
other women as well. A friend may make some vague allusion to
the anniversary of her breakup with her boyfriend and then get
angry that you didn't offer to go to dinner or a movie with her
that day. After the fact she might even say, "That was really
important to me and you didn't even notice." It's amazing how
assertive we can become in retrospect.

A valuable lesson for both getting along and getting ahead is
to state what you want when you want it. It can be terrifying
because it can mean meeting rejection head-on, but once you
start asking for what you want, it gets easier. When I decided to
leave my last nine-to-five job to sink or swim as a freelance writer,
my soon-to-be ex-employer asked if there was anything he could

do to assist in my new venture. I almost answered with the automatic, "Nothing, thank you," but instead I heard myself say, "You could lend me your apartment in New York when I go there next month to meet with editors."

I immediately felt my face get hot. I wanted to crawl under his big mahogany desk and disappear. It was no secret that he and his wife had an apartment in Manhattan, but for me as a lowly employee to ask for something so grand seemed ludicrously presumptuous. As I mentally measured the space beneath the desk to see how I'd fit, I heard my boss saying, "Excellent. We love it when that place is used." My daughter and I spent four wonderful days in an elegant studio overlooking Central Park, and I got three magazine assignments to propel my career as a freelancer.

Ask for what you want. You'll be amazed at how often you get a positive response. Ask politely and directly. "I know this is stupid and you really won't want to do it, but I was thinking maybe I'd ask anyway" is not a suitable preface. Just ask. Say "Thank you" for a yes and "Thanks anyway" for a no. When you're turned down, ask someone else, go through different channels, or find some alternative method for meeting your need.

Support the asking-and-receiving process by responding affirmatively to other people's requests as often as you can without neglecting your own life and your primary obligations. In addition to coming through for other people when they ask, you also contribute to the world at large every time you clearly and expectantly ask for what you want. This gives everybody within earshot permission to do the same.

32.

BECOME AN
UNHURRIED WOMAN

*An unhurried woman is willing to include some emptiness in
her day. That way, when you ask if she's got time for you,
she almost always does.*

The most crucial step toward creating a charmed life in this era of
epidemic busyness may well be to become an unhurried woman.
They do exist: I know several, and I do my best to emulate them.
Sherry is one of these. Remarkably, she also has a demanding life
as a nursing student and the mother of six children, including two
in college and two in diapers. She writes poetry and juvenile fiction, and gives presentations on midwifery and natural childbirth.
She manages the household on her husband's earnings as a hotel
waiter, and they arrange their schedules so everybody is home for
dinner and none of their children is ever in day care.

When I read about women like this, I think there's something left out: a congenial live-in grandmother, maybe, or a trust
fund funneling in extra cash. But in closely observing Sherry and
women who share her unhurried state, I believe their secret is neither household help nor supplemental income: it is simply that
they value serenity over stimulation. These women may be busy,
but they aren't driven. They refuse to be.

An unhurried woman holds her priorities sacrosanct. She

doesn't waste time trying to figure out where to invest her energies because she knows what takes precedence for her. An unhurried woman makes bold choices. Her life as a whole may include myriad involvements, but she wouldn't dare insert into any particular day more of them than she can comfortably handle. She is willing, in the spirit of St. Francis, to "do few things but do them well." She can get her to-do list on a Post-It. She's willing to include some emptiness in her day. That way, when you ask if she's got time for you, she almost always does.

Can we all become unhurried women? I think so—but we have to want it. Many of us who think we do really don't. It's difficult to go against the cultural notion that having a lot going on makes us worthy. When we believe that, we value ourselves only for what we *do*, thus denying who we *are*.

Of course, some of us truly like the excitement of being under the gun—"the rush of the rush." It can feel exhilarating to dash from one place to another, or converse with some important person while having two others on hold. We accessorize the madness with our pagers, appointment books, electronic organizers, and enough coffee to awaken a platoon. This is both a thrilling way to live and an easy way to lose touch with what we value most.

To take steps toward becoming an unhurried woman, first contemplate how you might feel if you weren't always rushing. Expect a variety of feelings: peace, emptiness, freedom, anxiety, relaxation, even—heaven forbid—boredom.

If, after surveying your possible emotional reactions to slowing down, you're brave enough to proceed, look at the day ahead of you. How packed is it? What can you eliminate or postpone to clear some space on your calendar? How can you accomplish what's left in an unhurried manner? Can you leave for work five minutes earlier so a red light won't be stressful? Can you think about tomorrow's dinner tonight when the pressure is off? Can you get some help? Maybe another mom can drive your kids to Scouts tomorrow since you drove hers last week.

It takes courage to become an unhurried woman. It means giving up accolades like "I don't know how she does it all." Those heady adrenaline surges will come less often. Friends still tied to an impossible schedule and an unforgiving clock will think you've sold out. You have. And you've come out ahead.

33.

SEEK COMPATIBLE
FREQUENCIES

"You have to find places where you recognize yourself."

We're happiest and most productive when surrounded by people and places that are in sync with us. I realized this some years ago when I moved to the country. I missed urban amenities, and I missed urban energy even more. Although the area where I lived was beautiful, I never felt like myself there. People so often told me I was a fish out of water that I thought I'd grown gills. "You have to find places where you recognize yourself," a wise friend said to me. In my case, those places of recognition include funky little theaters, grand old department stores, cozy coffee houses, and crowded buses.

Seeking out compatible frequencies doesn't mean keeping yourself away from anything different or unfamiliar. In fact, you can sometimes blissfully "recognize yourself" in a new friend or a foreign environment. Whether you're feeling that wonderful sense of ease in your backyard hammock, the café around the corner, or a street market in Beijing, you draw strength from being in your element.

Putting yourself in these situations is especially important in times of change. During life passages like a marriage, a move, a breakup, or a career shift, make a special point of finding places to recognize yourself. Visit the church you grew up in, even if you're affiliated with a different faith now. Read a book you loved when you read it the first time. Call a friend who knows how to listen and what to say.

Frequent places where you're a regular. There is comfort in having *your* post office, *your* newsstand, *your* hardware store. Stock your cupboards with your kind of food. Keep evidence of your life—crafts, photos, memorabilia—obvious in your home and office. If you wear cologne, choose a "signature fragrance." You don't have to wear it all the time—just enough that you identify with it. Then when you need a whiff of compatibility, you've got one.

A more serious way to respect your frequency is to stop expecting yourself to do things that are totally alien to your nature. I'm not suggesting that you refuse to perform necessary tasks—but when you have some say in the matter, you can save yourself from the square peg–round hole frustration of activities that are antagonistic to your essential self.

My first husband died when our daughter was four. I figured I had to be both mother and father then, so within a month of the funeral, I was in the park across from our apartment building attempting to play whiffle-ball with my child. It was a disaster. I was dreadful at it and grumpy about it. I learned in one afternoon that I could not revolutionize my being, even to fill a real need. Instead, I solicited other people to play ball with Rachael. Our free time together was spent reading aloud, doing art projects, and taking impromptu field trips to places we both found intriguing. The effort I could have put into being a poor excuse of a dad, I was able to direct toward being a really good mother.

We all have gifts. When we use them, we're at our best—and we're most comfortable. Tune to your compatible frequencies through your talents and interests, the people you know, and the places where you spend time. Recognize yourself in them. Relax. Make yourself at home. As you create the life you've always dreamed of, make sure it still looks like you.

34

STUDY METHOD ACTING

*The closer your actual living now comes to your
hoped-for living in the future, the more likely you are
to grow into your vision.*

You don't need theatrical aspirations to benefit from this acting method: the method of acting as if you already lived a charmed life. This is the fine art of faking it. It's not dishonest because you're not operating outside the truth, only outside the purview of present fact. Facts are malleable; they change all the time. You can help change them for the better.

First, think about what you want to do. What are your heart's desires? How would you like to improve your life? Now, imagine that it has already happened. Put yourself in that picture. If you were living in every way the life you want to live, what would you be wearing? What would you have eaten for breakfast this morning? What dishes would you have used? What would you be doing with this day? What would go on your to-do list?

As you answer these questions, consider the number of matchups you have between your existing life and your life in that idyllic, imagined tomorrow. The closer your actual living *now* comes to your hoped-for living in the future, the more likely you are to grow into your vision. Rehearse!

Get into costume. Start rehearsing for the life you want by looking like the person you want to be. If this sounds like dealing with the surface, that's because it is. How you look is not by a long shot who you are. But dressing the part can be the first phase in convincing yourself that it's really yours.

If in the imagination exercise you envisioned yourself in a designer suit, get one, even if it means going to a consignment shop or finding something out of season that's been marked down four times. Or maybe you plan on leaving the corporate grind to become a painter. Rehearse your future by dressing down all weekend and bringing out your paints and brushes.

Say your lines. The rest of the world believes what we tell it with our words, our actions, and our convictions. We like to think that other people's opinions don't matter, but that's only partially true. Other people's opinions make up our reputation. It's easier to live up to one we want than live down one we don't want.

Therefore, include your dream when you identify yourself. Tell people whatever aspects of your life you choose to reveal, but give star billing to the parts you're passionate about.

Become your character. After dressing and talking as if your dream were already here, live the lifestyle you aspire to as fully as you can within the parameters of your current reality. That way, when you're actually living the charmed life you envision, you won't be out of place. If, for instance, you want to have more money, subscribe to the *Wall Street Journal* and join an investment club. If you want to be a poet, go to readings. Hang out in bookstore coffee bars. Name your puppy Ginsberg.

Learn from the leads. Once you're looking, sounding, and seeming like someone whose dreams are taking shape, see your dreams in the flesh by getting to know people who are successfully doing what you want to do. Join the organizations they belong to. Sign up for the classes they teach and the conferences where they speak. Find out what they did to get where they are and apply those techniques that strike a chord with you.

Rehearse your dream—in costume, with lines, and as your character. Learn all you can from more experienced actors. Now, go break a leg.

35.

GROW THROUGH
THE HARD TIMES

"This isn't the end of the story. It's just a twist in the plot." Without remembering this, we can open ourselves to despair, to giving up.

All great people have gone through periods of reversal of fortune. Perhaps they lived through war or a financial depression; or personal crises made their lives look, at times, anything but charmed. When we look at these people's lives as a whole, we can see their cycles, the ups and downs, the successes and failures.

When it comes to our own life, it's easy to lose sight of the cyclic way of things. Rough times give us selective amnesia. Especially if we're having multiple struggles—work *and* relationship problems, or a health challenge along with money concerns—we tend to forget that we've been through hard stuff before. We've always survived, and sometimes we've triumphed.

My friend Crystal, blessed with a genius for perspective, has reminded me more than once, "This isn't the end of the story. It's just a twist in the plot." Without remembering this, we can open ourselves to despair, to giving up. Difficult times can last longer than they need to because we see them as permanent instead of transient.

You can also get into trouble when you too thoroughly identify with your circumstances. Body changes like those brought on by pregnancy or aging are harder for women who get their worth from the way they look. Financial reversals are more difficult for those who believe that they don't just *have* money but *are* their money. The more aware you can stay of who you really are—the eternal, unlimited essence of yourself—the easier it will be to deal with the conditions around you that fluctuate all the time.

Sometimes, accepting change seems to conflict with thinking positively. Expecting the best doesn't appear to allow for disappointments, downturns, and backward steps. But once you grasp the concept that life operates in a rhythmic, cyclic pattern, expecting the best includes expecting the pattern. The best—or even "the better"—can't come into your life by any other route.

When you're going through a trying time, accept as best you can that this is part of the pattern, part of a larger picture. Get the support you need while you're in it. Take the action you can to get through it. Look for this cloud's supposed silver lining, even when silver plate seems like a stretch. For all the aggravation change causes us, it is because change is always possible that hope is always appropriate.

36.

DON'T CRY OVER
SPILLED MILK

*Central to a life that works is forward motion.
Crying over spilled milk—with its accompanying
explanations, justifications, and confrontations—
is retrograde by definition.*

I can still hear my mother saying, "Don't cry over spilled milk." That advice means even more in adult affairs than it did at childhood breakfasts, because as adults we don't just *cry* over things that already happened—we try to *change* what already happened. Attempting to alter the past is frustrating because, whether you're dealing with something the magnitude of a milk spill or an oil spill, you can modify only its effects, not the event itself.

If you yourself spilled the milk, your honor depends on taking responsibility for what happened and making amends. Amends aren't just apologies: they're actions that actually make a difference, the way amendments to the Constitution are meant to alter and improve on the original document.

If somebody else was responsible for the spill, put it in perspective. How important is it? Will its effects be felt a year from now? If not, downplay your reaction. Some people exhibit the same level of emotion for every situation: four-alarm blaze. A charmed life demands that we discern intensity and respond appropriately.

It is wise to let some time elapse between the incident and your response to it. Let's say you find that the grocery sacker smashed the peaches with a forty-eight-ounce can of tomato juice. It's not exactly something to go to war over, but it can feel that way when you first pull out the surprise bag of pureed fruit. This is because we first experience what happens to us emotionally, and only later rationally. I'm embarrassed by the number of times I've been livid over something just that insignificant. Waiting an hour or a day before trying to do something about it would have spared me many meals of humble pie.

Doing some physical exercise can defuse an overreaction, and it helps shorten the waiting period between the event and reasonably responding to it. Expressing your aggravation on the phone with an understanding person can work well, too, as long as you talk with one or two people and stop. Half a dozen rehashes can unrealistically enlarge a minor offense.

Central to a life that works is forward motion. Crying over spilled milk—with its accompanying explanations, justifications, and confrontations—is retrograde by definition. Repair the past, whether distant or recent, when such reparation can make a positive difference in your present world or someone else's. Then turn your attention to the most important moment in your life: this one.

37.

BE SPECIFIC

*Being specific invites into your experience
what you really want.*

My favorite sentence in a whole book of wonderful sentences, Thomas Moore's *Care of the Soul*, is this: "The soul thrives on the particular and the vernacular." Reading that line was a watershed experience for me. I'd previously thought of the soul's concerns as nebulous and ethereal. The idea that my soul, the purest essence of myself, could flourish amid the goings-on of real life was a revelation.

The soul, the self, requires concreteness. There is comfort in knowing and acting on specifics. Whether you're the producer or receiver of ambiguity, it's annoying even in trivial situations. What do you do when a label says "Hand wash in cold water. May be machine washed, gentle cycle. For best results, dry clean"? There's nothing left except "Take to river, pound on stone."

In weightier matters, vagueness is more disconcerting. "My kid needs so much money for college!" is horrifying, because "so much" could be synonymous with "infinite." To say, "I want to provide fifty thousand dollars for my child's education" may be daunting, but it's freeing, too. You now have something solid to shoot for instead of something uncertain to fret over.

Being specific also invites into your experience what you really want. Lots of women are more definite when ordering bedclothes from a catalog than when "ordering" a career or life partner from the universe. No one would send for a set of sheets and say, "Twin, queen, whatever you've got," but the divine fulfillment service, interpreting our mental yearnings, gets countless requests as unclear as "I'd really like a job," and "It would be awfully nice to have a husband." It's no wonder so many people are living lives that don't fit: they've requisitioned their circumstances without ever specifying a size or description.

It takes courage to be specific, because it implies that we won't settle for just anything. Without being precise about what we want, what we expect, and what we are willing to accept, we open ourselves to potluck.

Unless you want to worry half the night, you don't tell a teenager to be home early; you say, "eleven o'clock." If you like the length of your hair, you don't ask your hairdresser to cut "just a little"; you say, "half an inch." If you don't want to stew over never getting your way, minimize your use of namby-pamby phrases like "It's up to you" and "It doesn't matter." If it truly doesn't matter, fine, but don't let shyness, indecisiveness, or lack of confidence relegate you to the limbo of "whatever."

Just for practice, for the next month answer questions like "Do you want smoking or nonsmoking?" with one or the other, but not "Either way." When the taxi driver asks if you want to go via the bridge or the tunnel, say "Bridge" or "Tunnel." When the ticket agent asks your preference for an aisle or window seat, have one. Be flexible, of course: if the only seat left is in the center, you don't have to demand to speak to a supervisor. You've stated your preference. If you then voluntarily accept something else, you've made a choice to be gracious and adaptable.

As you develop the grit to be more precise in your own speech and intentions, acquire some extra mettle for facing the facts life presents to you in their unadorned and non-watered-down state. Ask direct questions like "How much do I owe?" and "Exactly what do you want me to do?" Expect direct answers. Engage in direct action. Expect a life of more clarity, certainty, and peace.

38.

DECIDE THAT YOU'RE BEAUTIFUL

The secret is to decide that you're beautiful already. . . .
Once you do, other people will believe it too.

Okay, beauty is fleeting, skin deep, and to the people who love us it doesn't matter anyway. We all know that. We also know that attractive people get perks. Studies show that teachers favor good-looking students, supervisors favor good-looking employees, and when little children are asked to pick the "strangers" from a group of photographs, they choose the less attractive people for that ominous distinction.

Although the obsession with physical appearance affects everyone in our culture, women are more victimized by it than men. As a result, many articulate voices decry this overblown emphasis and make convincing cases for change. In the meantime, great-looking people have an undeniable advantage. I find that the most sensible answer to this apparent inequity is to be a great-looking person.

This is not just a glib comment. With very few exceptions, any woman of any age or body type can do it. The secret is to decide that you're beautiful already. A watershed experience for me came years ago in meeting an actress known as a great beauty. She confided in me, "I'm not really beautiful. I just realized when

I was very young that my life would be better if I were, so I decided I would be. That's the impression I've given ever since."

Her revelation gave me permission to stop seeing myself as pudgy, with bad skin and the wrong kind of hair, and instead let my inner beauty show on the outside too. You may have already figured out a way to do this that works for you. If not, help yourself to mine:

Decide that you're beautiful. Let your quirks and imperfections be part of your beauty, like the models who turn a mole or a gap between their front teeth into a trademark. Keep reminding yourself that you're beautiful until you believe it. Once you do, other people will believe it too. When you get a compliment, accept it.

Ignore society's fickle standards and celebrate your unique brand of beauty. Roberta, a friend I've had since high school, has thick, curly hair, a wide, sensuous smile, and a voluptuous figure. In the era of ironed hair, invisible lips, and Twiggy, she was a miserable teenager, but in her twenties, she wised up. When we were shopping for party clothes one day, she selected a dress that emphasized her already enviable cleavage. "You make the most of what you've got," she said, flashing me that dazzling smile. Roberta chose to be beautiful. Eventually, the culture caught up.

Groom yourself religiously. Whether your style is a candlelight bath with perfumed oils or a soap and water shower, start every day freshly scrubbed and smelling good. Keep your haircut current. Get your teeth cleaned on schedule. Take care of your nails, fingers and toes. Tend to loose buttons, beginning rips, and scuffed shoes as if you had a valet.

Get healthy. "Health and beauty," wrote Emerson, "are nature's gifts for living within her laws." Exercise, rest, and nutritious food are the raw materials for clear skin, sparkling eyes, shiny hair, and a strong, supple physique. And taking care of yourself physically makes you *feel* beautiful from the outset (see Secret 55, "Boost Your Vitality").

Find your style. Maybe you love fashion and make-up; or maybe you thrive on wearing jeans and showing the world your unadorned face. Either can be beautiful. Find your style by making note of how you look when you feel most like yourself. You can dress up or down for specific occasions, but your basic style— romantic, tailored, exotic, whatever—will stay with you. Then you'll always feel comfortable about how you look, so you can forget about it and focus on what's really going on.

Don't get stuck. Some women get caught in a time warp: they pick a year and look like that for the rest of their lives. Without being a slave to trends, let your look gradually evolve to reflect the woman you are today.

Polish your soul. If you're healthy, well-groomed, and think well of your physical self, you'll look good, but to be truly beautiful, you have to be lit from within. This amazing, ageless glow comes from inside. Start with some quiet time (see Secret 5, "Take Ten"); it will do as much for your face as a standing appointment at Elizabeth Arden. Do work you believe in, whether it's for love or money. Play with abandon. And smile a lot, so when you get lines on your face, they'll point up.

39.

FORM A

MASTERMIND ALLIANCE

*Surprising power is generated when a group of individuals
see one another's futures as exceedingly bright.*

If you intend to hitch your wagon to a star, enlist the aid of a
driver, a blacksmith, and an astronomer. Well-chosen people will
not only support and encourage you; they'll act as conduits and
connections to get you where you're going.

When you depend on your own experience, you've got
what—thirty years' worth? Forty? What if you joined with peers
to form a mastermind alliance, a gathering of kindred spirits dedicated to helping one another make everyone's dreams come
true? Let's see, half a dozen people, thirty-five years of age on
average—you're looking at 210 years of on-the-job training in
mastering life on earth.

Every Tuesday morning I meet with several other women for
breakfast. As self-employed speakers and writers, our original
intention was to support each other professionally. As it turns out,
we also support each other personally. Even when we're floun-
dering one at a time, we have as a group tremendous wisdom and
insight. We expect great things from one another, and each of us
in turn meets the others' expectations.

The host at the restaurant calls ours "the tea table," since we drink more tea than coffee, and he has our corner spot ready every week. For the first seven months we met, we had a server named Fran. She made sure there was always Earl Grey in the tea chest, and she kept track of which of us didn't want blueberries on her oatmeal.

One summer morning, Fran was beaming. "All these months," she told us, "I've been overhearing you ladies encourage one another, and I started to realize I could be doing more with my life too. I got up my nerve to apply to a restaurant management program. They accepted me and I'll start next week."

Fran's metamorphosis is telling, because it was the result of "sidestream mentoring." She wasn't officially part of the mastermind process, but she was able to change her life from being aware of bits and pieces of it. Surprising power is generated when a group of individuals see one another's futures as exceedingly bright.

Mastermind relationships do not usurp or undermine connections to partner and family, but they do take some of the pressure off. It can be burdensome for a spouse, for instance, to be the only one with whom we share our doubts and anxieties about everything from the promotion we want to the haircut we can't stand. The mentors and confidantes in a mastermind alliance can take up some of the slack.

You can form a mastermind circle with as few as three members, although a larger number—six to eight—is ideal. That way, when sick kids, business trips, and flat tires intervene, there will still be enough of you for a viable get-together.

You can create the circle from your close friends, but the

most effective groups are often comprised of people who aren't well acquainted at the outset but instead share a goal, a vision, or a lifestyle. Women in the same profession, mothers with children of similar ages, or members of a particular religious faith can have enough in common to gather with a shared purpose even before strong friendships develop.

Our group formed because we were fairly new members of a professional organization. The old guard had mastermind groups of their own already, so we were assembled by default. But few things happen by blind chance, and we turned out to have uncanny similarities. We were in the right group, default or not.

Once you have assembled your circle, decide how often you'll meet, where, and what parameters you'll set. It is helpful to have some ground rules—for instance, you might have an understanding that everyone will get a chance to speak without interruption or comment unless she asks for feedback. Such gentle boundaries maintain focus.

Most important, everyone in the group must be committed to supporting everyone else. This is no place for jealousy or rivalry. In your mastermind alliance, you'll need to be like the Three Musketeers, "all for one and one for all." You will certainly have the opportunity to offer advice, counsel, and information within the group, but your primary obligation is to see every other member growing, stretching, and becoming more and more the person she wants to be. When you have a circle of friends believing in you this much, it's like running your life on high-octane fuel. You can count on improved performance.

40.

DELIGHT IN DETAILS

When we fail to relish details, it's tempting to succumb to greed and discontent. Without the joy of tiny things, we want more and bigger ones.

We set our goals based on the big picture, but our joy comes from the details. A charmed life is populated with particulars that touch you in a way that's personal and distinctive. It's important to invite in the details you know make you happy, and stay open to delicious details that show up unexpectedly. Not long ago I bought a crocheted cloche hat at a backstreet boutique. I welcomed the hat as a lovely detail—it's becoming, works well with my haircut, and reminds me of my favorite era, the 1920s. But the greater happiness from the purchase came after I got it home: when I opened the little beige bag with handles, I found my new hat wrapped in tissue paper the color of a walnut brownie.

I like tissue paper anyway—it reminds me of birthday gifts and the taffeta dresses of my childhood coming out of their boxes. And brown tissue paper! This was a surprise like coming upon brown ink as a teenager when I thought blue and black were the only choices, and discovering brown bread after growing up on the pasty white kind.

I took the brown tissue paper and flattened it beneath *Paintings in the Louvre, Gone With the Wind*, and both volumes of a not-so-abridged dictionary. Then I folded it lengthwise and put it in my box of wrapping materials in the company of satin ribbons, hand-stamped papers, and silver cord. I will pass it along for someone else's delight.

When we fail to relish details, it's tempting to succumb to greed and discontent. Without the joy of tiny things, we want more and bigger ones. As the quantity of our possessions increases, we tend to lose the details, and we can find ourselves with less and less that speaks to our hearts.

Train yourself to see the details of your life the way a photographer looks for the details of a scene. But don't stop with what you see: use all your senses to become a connoisseur of events and details. For example, a great lunch is an event; that it came on a plate painted with poppies is a detail. Event: visiting a longtime friend. Detail: blowing bubbles with her two-year-old. Event: walking to work. Detail: feeding what's left of your bagel to a couple of brazen pigeons.

Don't keep your appreciation of details to yourself. Point out the wild strawberries barely visible in the grass, the gargoyles atop an otherwise nondescript apartment building, the way the air today smells like London after a rain. And surround yourself with people who understand the importance of a nearly unnoticeable item or interlude. Because society at large applauds the big, the noisy, and the obvious, it's helpful to have in your personal world others who value the small, the quiet, and the subtle. Someone once said, "God is in the details." So are most of the pleasures of life.

41.

PROSPER

For a grounded sense of self in this era and culture,
we need to be financially skid-proof.

Women are making momentous strides economically, but it still seems to me that more women than men are uncomfortable with money. Both "filthy rich" and "dirt poor" are incompatible with "sugar and spice and everything nice," so many of us have avoided thinking about money in favor of taking whatever comes via the path of least resistance. As a result, we may be enchanted with what money can buy but intimidated by its acquisition and upkeep. For a grounded sense of self in this era and culture, we need to be financially skid-proof.

If money is an issue, time that could be spent cultivating an exceptional life will go instead to working overtime, worrying overtime, and wearing yourself out to come up with ingenious ways to pay off your MasterCard with your Visa. Like the other aspects of our lives, however, financial well-being depends on living in accord with underlying principles. The ones I know are these:

Money is nothing to be afraid of. Get comfortable with it. Carry some extra cash so you'll never be without it. Balance your checkbook promptly. Pay your bills on time. Know how much you have and how much you owe. Enjoy your money without anxiety. It's only zeros.

Spend joyfully but rationally. Some people use purchasing power to make up for feeling powerless otherwise, but reckless spending fuels further helplessness. Buy what you need and buy what makes your heart sing. Respect yourself, your space, and your solvency enough to leave the rest in the store.

Be wary of debt. You rob your future when you spend money you don't have by using credit without reserve cash or collateral to cover the purchase. Unless you conscientiously pay off credit cards each month, consider the freedom of a cash economy, incurring no unsecured debt. (An invaluable guide is *How to Get Out of Debt, Stay Out of Debt, and Live Prosperously,* by Jerrold Mundis.)

Give some of your money away. Giving makes receiving possible. Giving regularly to something you believe in can both make you feel good and actually increase your own prosperity. When you give money away, you feel rich. Everybody knows the rich get richer. People who practice tithing, contributing 10 percent of all after-tax income to their church or to charity, say they no longer worry about money, what they have goes farther, and more flows in from unexpected sources.

Put some of your money aside. Compound interest is a wonder of the world. If saving is hard for you, start with a small but consistent automatic transfer from your paycheck or checking account into a money market or mutual fund. As your money grows *for* you, saving will grow *on* you.

It doesn't pay to deprive yourself. The opposite of squandering, deprivation leads to discontent, self-pity, and periodic spending binges. Instead, use your resources to take good care of yourself as well as those you love. As long as you're not going into debt to do it, treat yourself to fulfilling experiences and guilt-free gifts.

Appreciate what you have. More people complain about what they're missing than marvel at having a standard of living that represents the pinnacle of human achievement—a standard of living you and I both have. By global standards, the difference in lifestyle between us and the Sultan of Brunei is insignificant. Gratitude is called for.

Learn prosperity principles and the basics of finance. To make friends with a person, you find out about her life and her interests. To make friends with money, do the same thing. Read the financial pages. Take a course in consumer economics. Learn about the metaphysical underpinnings of abundance.

Have enough. Living simply is a choice. Living in lack is a problem. Believe in your worth and the value of what you do. It isn't easy to negotiate a fee or a salary (see Secret 31, "Ask for What You Want") or leave a comfortable position for something better, but the payoff, emotionally and financially, can be enormous.

Don't limit abundance. Abundance is fullness of life, not numbers on a ledger. Rich is relative. For one woman, it's a high-paying job, an impressive house, and exotic travel. For another, it's going to part-time work, one car, and an in-state vacation in exchange for the wealth of having more time with her kids. Be rich your way. You'll feel like a million bucks.

42.

CULTIVATE COMPASSION

*Every person you see has stories, and every person you see
has a few that would break your heart. We deserve each
other's respect simply because we've survived all
we have and kept going anyway.*

It has been said, "He who lives for himself alone lives for the meanest mortal known." Compassion expands us. It extends our scope of positive influence beyond our immediate situation. Any success is hollow without it.

The literal definition of compassion is "to feel with." It means living with the knowledge that your life is as important as mine, your dreams as valid, your children as precious, your pain as real. Compassion gives us a more valid view of the world by taking us out of its center. Every person you see has stories, and every person you see has a few that would break your heart. We deserve each other's respect simply because we've survived all we have and kept going anyway.

Compassion fuels kindness, gentleness, and patience. It helps you realize that everybody else is doing the best they can, just as you are. That makes it easier to give other imperfect people the benefit of the doubt. Compassion is also an invaluable aid in accepting others as they are and allowing them to be different from us.

Enhance your compassion by starting close to home, with yourself. We can be so hard on ourselves. Find the midpoint between putting yourself down and rationalizing mistakes away. Accept responsibility, but don't waste time with guilt. Treat yourself as you would a treasured friend.

Go from showing more compassion toward yourself to showing more compassion to those closest to you. These are the people we love so dearly that feeling their pain splits us in two. Love without compassion, however, gets twisted. It results in emotional oddities like feeling angry because loved ones aren't happy, or letting our fear of losing them overshadow their needs for growth, experience, and self-determination.

The next step is to express more compassion toward other people in your world, listening and helping out inasmuch as you're able. A little thoughtfulness goes a long way. But avoid overextending yourself for others; misappropriated compassion can deplete your resources, thereby short-circuiting the process.

Also be on guard for overextending as you go beyond those you know to express compassion to those you don't. There is no shortage of suffering. The sheer magnitude of it can make us want to retreat back into the comfort of more agreeable circumstances. One way to protect yourself while allowing your compassion to grow is to choose one cause that speaks to you and support it actively with your labor, your capital, or both. That way, you can know that even though you can't save the world, you can make a difference in one piece of it.

Finally, let your compassion go beyond the boundaries of human need to encompass other creatures too. "Until he extends the circle of his compassion to all living things," wrote Dr. Albert Schweitzer, "man will not himself find peace." Become conversant with the notion that there really is a majestic web of life and that all members of it hold their own lives dear.

Follow your compassion where it takes you, even though some people are bound to disapprove. Perhaps your cause isn't theirs, or the suffering that pierces your soul doesn't seem real to them, or they're simply so involved with their own concerns that little else matters. Save some compassion for them, too.

43.

DANCE WITH
YOUR SHADOW

*Our shadow can seem ugly at first glance, but there is
tremendous potential latent within all the risks we haven't
taken and all the adventures we haven't allowed ourselves.*

Dancing is a delightful way to get to know someone. It's intimate but safe. If you don't like the impression you get from one dance partner, it's perfectly acceptable to go on to another. In the same way, we can get to know more of who we are when we're willing to dance with that part of ourselves we usually turn away from, the component of the human psyche that psychologists call our "shadow" or "dark" side.

It sounds sinister, but our shadow side is dark only because we've never turned a light on it. If we did, we would see neglected talents and abandoned dreams, as well as an assortment of the things our parents disapproved of. We would find ideas that were too new, situations that were too frightening, and concepts that were too challenging for us to act on when they originally came up. Efficiently dispatched to our shadow side, these make it a reservoir of untapped power and promise—power and promise you can draw on for creating your charmed life. Nevertheless, years of suppressing both terrors and treasures in the same mental compartment make looking at any of it a daunting prospect.

I had an architectural illustration of the so-called dark side when my husband and I found our wonderful old house. We loved its roominess, the native stone, and the big windows, but it had a basement that could have been designed by Henry VIII. It was damp, dark, and dirty. Amid the debris we found a 1918 newspaper—evidence that few brave souls had ventured into this pit since the Armistice. I figured that, other than seeing to the occasional tripped circuit-breaker, we, too, could avoid this sub-terranean embarrassment.

My husband, however, was musing, "You know, we could turn this into a playroom—dry it out, scrape off the old paint, do the walls and ceilings white, and paint the pipes bright colors. We can put a basketball court here and gymnastics mats on this side, a TV over there, a game table against that wall. . . ." To my aston-ishment, two months of labor and eighteen gallons of dry-lock paint turned that erstwhile dungeon into the brightest, most pop-ular room in the house.

Like that bleak basement, our shadow can seem ugly at first glance, but there is tremendous potential latent within all the risks we haven't taken and all the adventures we haven't allowed ourselves. They're waiting inside us to be discovered and trans-formed—or to turn brown and crumble like an old newspaper.

What do you have tucked away in the dark? A talent for art some teacher once said wouldn't "get you anywhere"? The dream of a trip to Rome your first husband convinced you that you could never afford and weren't worth anyway? Put on some music and do some figurative dancing with your shadow. Consider what's been hiding there. Touch it—but don't get too close. This is a dance, not a marriage. You're getting to know a part of yourself that's been a stranger until now. It's appropriate to proceed slowly.

Once you feel comfortable with your dark side, you'll be operating as a more fully functioning human being. Your sunny self won't have to run things on her own. She'll have the backing and encouragement of a strong and fascinating partner. And in this dance, you always get to lead.

44.

RAISE YOUR AWE AND WONDER QUOTIENT

Self-esteem is the result of recognizing our personal power; awe and wonder come from recognizing our lack of it. Both are true, and in an exceptional life there is no conflict between them.

When we mentally catalog the things we think we want (more money, more recognition, a higher metabolic rate), the list rarely includes "I want more wonder." We seldom realize that we need a heightened sense of wonder more than any of that other stuff—and that if we had the wonder, we'd either get the rest with far less effort, or just feel so good it wouldn't matter.

People who live charmed lives are routinely wonderstruck. They say, "This is the best meal I ever had . . . the most adorable baby I ever saw . . . the most incredible concept I ever heard." They're not thoughtlessly exaggerating: it really seems that way to them.

Many of the secrets of charmed living relate to confidence, competence, and self-assurance, but awe and wonder are different. They come from what we don't understand and cannot reproduce. Self-esteem is the result of recognizing our personal power; awe and wonder come from recognizing our lack of it. Both are true, and in an exceptional life there is no conflict between them.

Once we were all experts at awe and wonder. That was a long time ago. The magic of early childhood—fairies under toadstools, invisible playmates, guardian angels—is, in a child's experience, as real as picking up the morning paper is to an adult. Awe will get you magic as surely as coins in a kiosk will get you the news of the day.

Anyone who wants this magic can get it back. Start by making room for mystery. Don't educate yourself out of the elation of being genuinely amazed. Unless you plan to be a magician, for instance, don't ask how the tricks are done. Let yourself ponder them instead. Albert Einstein himself said, "He who can no longer pause to wonder and stand rapt in awe, is as good as dead."

Next, avoid excesses in your life. A lot of the wonder you'll experience comes from sensual pleasure that is exquisite simply because it isn't an everyday occurrence. My friend Ann was at a travel writers' conference when participants were asked to share their most spiritual experience in traversing the globe. Ann replied without delay: "Eating bread pudding at Captain's Table in New Orleans." If she ate that bread pudding every day, or had ordered it after a seven-course meal, the experience wouldn't have been nearly as sublime.

Finally, observe with care the life around you. Few people observe. We see. Sometimes we even look. But thoughtful, focused observation can't take place in a hurry, or if you're afraid of being bored. Therefore, competence in observation is found largely among artists, scientists, and children. My twelve-year-old stepdaughter Siãn is a master of it. In recounting an event, she describes all the particulars: every sight, every smell, every conversational nuance.

When you can observe with that kind of presence, you engage with the majesty of the moment. Start your observation practice by observing nature. Nature deficiency is epidemic nowadays, but when you pause to observe it, you'll discover its peerless ability to activate your wonder faculty. Observe flowers, storms, rainbows, cloud formations, sunrises, sunsets, rocks, weeds, puddles, birds, insects, fallen leaves, spiderwebs, and especially stars.

I was once chatting with Talane Miedaner, a business and life coach in New York, about how I loved her city but couldn't understand why some New Yorkers seemed to think there was no life beyond Manhattan. "I know why that is," she said. "People lose perspective when they can't see the stars." It makes sense. Of course, you could be in Montana where stars proliferate, and without observing them, you'd never know that.

Look up. Look around. Observe. Avoid excess. Make room for mystery. Find at least one reason every day for saying, "Ahhh."

45.

ADD A LITTLE ROMANCE

*A charmed life is always romantic, whether you're single
and celibate or head-over-heels in love. Romance isn't
waiting for somebody else to leave roses at your door;
it's living with finesse and selectivity.*

When I get my hair cut, I read men's magazines—*Esquire*, *GQ*,
Men's Health—to see how the other half thinks. The main difference between men's magazines and women's magazines is that
those for men have almost no articles on relationships while the
ones for women are full of them.

Women seem to be especially wired for relating. Most of us
get energy from communicating with other people, working in
cooperation with them, and correlating our experiences with
theirs. A romantic relationship is the pièce de résistance of all this
relating. We get to be mirrored, validated, and cherished.

For a life charmed enough to weather the storms of romance,
our propensity for partnering has to come under the auspices of
the higher purpose. True partnership is just another way to shrink
the ego and enlarge the soul. From this vantage point, getting
married is no different from entering a convent, except for the
celibacy part.

When two people truly want to give to each other, grow
together, and become more as a couple than either could be sep-
arately, the resulting relationship is strong and self-renewing. It

will never be perfect, but sharing your life with someone who has your best interests at heart can be awfully sweet. You're most likely to get a relationship like that by creating a life for yourself that is full already. This is true if you're looking for a relationship or if you're already in one that you wish were better. The attraction between love and life is the archetype for all good relationships. When you're in love, your life sparkles. It works the other way, too: when your life is rich and full and thriving, love often shows up.

We come from love. It's what we're made of. Learning to love more fully is probably our most important life assignment. Romantic love gets complicated because of sex. We don't know what to do with something capable of producing ecstasy, so we diminish much of its beauty with guilt and embarrassment, excess and deprivation. That shouldn't be surprising: we've done the same thing to chocolate.

To allow a commodity as potentially combustible as romance into a charmed life requires practicing an enlightened version of safe sex: not just the good-sense stuff like condoms and monogamy, but a genuine respect for this extraordinary power within us. Some people claim to engage in casual sex, but to a woman's soul there is no such thing.

Honoring your sexual expression is one part of the equation. Honoring yourself when you're not in a relationship is the other. You can use the time when there is not a romantic partner in your life to fall more deeply in love with yourself and with God. The metaphor of romantic love and the soul's quest for the divine is found in almost every religion and mythology. This is the ultimate relationship and the most satisfying. Although being single in a doubled-up world is not easy, cultivating your spiritual side when you're on your own can give your life an otherwise unattainable depth and richness.

Moreover, a charmed life is always romantic, whether you're single and celibate or head-over-heels in love. Romance isn't waiting for somebody else to leave roses at your door; it's living with finesse and selectivity. It's romantic to stay in a quaint bed-and-breakfast instead of the standard chain hotel when you travel on business. It's romantic to spray fragrance on the sheets, even when you're sleeping alone. It's romantic to read poetry to yourself or to your cat. Most of all, it's romantic to live with great expectations.

In the meantime, love lavishly. Love your family, your friends, your work, your life. You know about *being* in love. This is *living* in love.

46.

RECRUIT SOLUTIONS
THAT WORK

Keep a roster of your proven strategies for feeling better. . . .
Just doing something can break the doom-and-gloom cycle.

If you think of it, you already have at your disposal a cadre of solutions to use when you're feeling down. You've called on them before, and they work. They suit you and the circumstances of your life.

When we're feeling glum, we often say, "I don't know what to do," but many remedies are interchangeable. The same actions you took to feel better when you were laid off last year will be just as effective sometime when you feel overwhelmed by work and melancholy from three straight days of an icy drizzle.

During periods like these, lethargy is our greatest enemy. We often don't do anything because nothing seems worth doing. Lifting a finger feels like lifting a barbell, but it's precisely what we need to do: just doing *something* can break the doom-and-gloom cycle.

I suggest keeping a roster of your proven strategies for feeling better. Don't overwhelm yourself. A short list is fine, eight to fifteen readily available, generally affordable things to do when you feel pathetic. ("Take a cruise" probably shouldn't be here. You want something you can do right away.)

Copy your list, put one in your bedroom and others in the kitchen, in your car, and in your desk at work. The reason for all the copies is that when you're feeling down, you're likely to forget that anything has ever helped bring your spirits up. Keeping your list near all the places you're apt to be means you're likely to see it even when you're not looking for it.

Be sure it contains only tactics that have a track record of coming through for you. With that caveat, I'll give you my list simply as a jump start for remembering proven strategies of your own:

Get together with a positive friend. A phone call is better than nothing, but making the effort to actually meet for coffee or a walk is considerably more effective.

Go to a funny movie, or an inspiring one. Note the words *go to;* watching a video is a remote second choice. The act of getting out is itself therapeutic. And for me, being in a dark theater with a big screen puts all my obligations on hold. For those two hours, my function is to immerse myself in a story, laugh out loud, or cry real tears.

Play show tunes. Broadway shows combine exhilarating lyrics with stirring music. I cannot remain dejected if I play "Hold On" from *Beauty and the Beast*, "Into the Fire" from *The Scarlet Pimpernel*, or "Only You" from *Starlight Express*.

Do free writing. Free writing, or writing in a journal, can mean letting feelings flood a piece of paper in a great, gushing torrent. Once they're out, you're likely to feel much better. If you write for long enough, practical solutions can surface that you didn't know you had in you (see Secret 50, "Keep a Journal").

Head for the gym. I'm not someone who really likes working out, but if I get myself around all those mirrors and stair-climbers and other people's energy, I feel better. Once I actually exert myself, endorphins—the body's feel-good chemicals that exercise releases—intensify and perpetuate the upswing.

Straighten a room. Creating order in my environment somehow creates order in my psyche. It doesn't have to be a whole room. Sometimes organizing a desk drawer is sufficient to pull me from a slump.

Use these and suggestions you hear from other people to prime the pump of your own inventiveness. Just don't wait until you need your list to make it. Do that now. Put it in places you can't help but find it. It should help you to more blue skies and fewer blue funks.

47.

ACKNOWLEDGE ALL
BLESSINGS

*Whether you think of it as giving thanks
or doing a reality check, counting your blessings maintains
a charmed life as surely as monthly touch-ups
maintain your hair color.*

Sometimes we get so busy pursuing our dream that we forget to notice the degree to which we're living it already. We compound our frustration by measuring our level of success or happiness against someone else's. We compare our insides to their outsides.

My friend Denise was lamenting a litany of woes to her manicurist. The woman finally stopped filing, took Denise's soaking hand out of the soapy water, and looked her straight in the eye. "Denise," she implored, "Don't you know you're the woman the rest of us want to be?"

It makes you wonder why psychologists get paid more than manicurists. That pronouncement across the table did more for Denise than a posthumous session with Carl Jung would have. It momentarily freed her from her first-person vantage point so she could see from what fiction writers call universal perspective. She was able in that instant to get an idea of how her life looked to the rest of the world: pretty darn good.

Whether you think of it as giving thanks or doing a reality

check, counting your blessings maintains a charmed life as surely as monthly touch-ups maintain your hair color. (All right: *my* hair color.) A blessing is anything that's wonderful, anything that's okay, or anything that's not as bad as it used to be or as bad as it might be. We're tripping over them all the time.

Other people's blessings can look better than ours, the way that whatever your date orders for dinner almost always looks better than what you're having. Because most of us were brought up with a scarcity mindset, it can seem that every time somebody else gets extravagant recognition, a dream trip, or even a bargain on a pair of shoes, the universe is playing favorites. It doesn't work that way; the blessings bank is not overseen by Ebenezer Scrooge. Get a truer picture of the way things are by looking at your life as if it were someone else's.

Try this exercise: Write down one blessing you can see in each of the various areas of your life. Write one thing about your family that's positive. Write one thing about your finances that's really good. Write one thing that's going well regarding your home, your work, your health, your hobby, your education, your car, your looks, your talents, your friends, and your day.

Your list may start something like "My mom takes the kids on Saturday nights. . . . I put $100 a month in an IRA. . . . My apartment has nice hardwood floors. . . . My new boss respects what I do. . . . My cholesterol is only 138 . . ." Now look at your list as if it belonged to another person. "*Her* mother babysits. . . . *She* saves $100 a month. . . . *She's* got fabulous floors, a great boss, and exemplary arteries." It's easier to see your life as the deluxe model when you think of someone else living it.

Hold on to this enlightened view of your own experience by taking a pause from time to time simply to be grateful. It's fine—desirable even—to be appropriately awestruck by the fact that you earned a degree, or that your granddaughter did; that you grew from the shyest kid in your high school into a self-possessed late bloomer; or that the cat you rescued off the street on a whim has been your stalwart friend for thirteen years.

I don't know the precise mechanics by which blessings enter our lives, but I do know that acknowledging the ones we have brings in more. And the divine forces that play a part must appreciate it when we notice.

48.

CHOOSE ACTUAL OVER VIRTUAL REALITY

It is more important than ever to indulge ourselves, as well as any children we influence, in living books, live music, and unfiltered nature.

A charmed life grows out of real experiences and real relationships. These can be at a premium in our age of virtual reality, when images routinely stand in for the actual. Computers call you up and pretend to be people. Pieces of plastic pretend to be money. Chemicals pretend to be food.

Despite the proliferation of ersatz reality, we still appreciate the genuine article. That's why people stand in long lines and pay dearly to get tickets for actual events, whether operas, rock concerts, or football games, even if they could see them for nothing on TV.

More than a century before technology was able to mutate reality with the sophistication and thoroughness it does today, a British teacher named Charlotte Mason developed a philosophy of education based on life experience and what she called "living books." A living book, fiction or nonfiction, is one that puts the reader in touch with vital thoughts and events. Boring, poorly written books, as well as texts that fail to energize facts with the ideas behind them, she called "twaddle." Until children become inured to twaddle—which today is heaped upon them electronically as well as in print—they recognize it and put it on par with pureed liver.

When my daughter was six, she announced that she wanted to read the Bible. I said, "You'd like to read some Bible stories. Okay, we'll get a book."

"Not Bible stories," she said, "I want to read the Bible." So we started where it starts, "In the beginning . . ." I didn't think she'd last through the first set of "begats," but with some explanation, she showed a surprising ability to take in the lofty ideals and lovely poetry. Other parents have told me similar stories about their children's excitement over Shakespeare, Rembrandt, or Beethoven. For someone young or old, this kind of beauty can bypass the intellect and go straight to the soul.

In our era of twaddle run rampant, it is more important than ever to indulge ourselves, as well as any children we influence, in living books, live music, and unfiltered nature. Spend some time outside every day, especially if you work in an environment in which the only windows are the ones on your computer screen. Eat more food that grew and less that was manufactured. Wear natural-fiber clothing so your pores can breathe.

In addition, touch reality through your creativity and the creative works of others. Wherever you live, there are painters, potters, silversmiths, and woodworkers who produce wares as alive in their own way as the living books Charlotte Mason praised. In addition to artists and craftspeople, farmers who respect the land, merchants who respect their customers, and physicians who respect their patients are all involved in the real and the important. Help bring into being the world you want by supporting those who hold a similar vision.

If, for example, you find that shopping at the last corner grocery store in town is a rendezvous with real life that the fluorescent-lit, stadium-sized supermarket can't match, by all means shop there. It may not be open all night or have seventy-nine varieties of dry cereal, but the owner is liable to save a bone for your dog and order in any cereal you ask for.

Finally, take a stand for reality by playing an active part in it. There's a saying that goes "Some people make things happen. Others watch things happen. The rest wonder what happened." The watchers are rapidly outnumbering both other groups, but real life is participatory. It balances consumption with production. And when you leave it there's less regret, because you know without any doubt that you were here.

49

COOPERATE WITH BENEVOLENCE

Look for the good—in yourself and all around you. Positive thinking may not be a panacea, but it is the most basic way we have to cooperate with benevolence.

It doesn't take any more time to think in a way that makes your life better than it does to think in a way that makes your life miserable. People whose inner spirit spills over into their lives in the real world look for the good, and their days flow smoothly most of the time. When you ask how they are and they tell you they're fine, they mean it. This isn't the kind of positive thinking that's regimented and enforced, but simply a nod to the good given often enough that it becomes natural.

We tend to get what we look for. But just as it's easier to let our bodies sag than to exercise consistently, it's easier to let our thinking slump into negativity than to jog it up to something better. Some will even argue that there are certain benefits to awaiting doomsday: if it doesn't happen, you get to feel terrific. There's also a kind of superstition around expecting something awful and somehow willing the dreaded event away. You could think of it as prophylactic worry.

Nevertheless, truly spiritual people and truly happy people (those particular demographic groups tend to overlap) expect the best to the point of annoying everyone else. It's even more annoying when marvelous things keep happening for them, which they generally do. The point is to learn how to be just as annoying as they are.

From a purely mathematical viewpoint, you're better off expecting a positive outcome, because that's what usually happens. Life has a vested interest in perpetuating itself. Therefore, it tends to come through for its participants the majority of the time. This is not to deny the existence of delay, disappointment, loss, and sadness. Even these, however, when you can stand apart and view them in retrospect, are often part of a progression toward greater good.

Help yourself get comfortable with expecting the good by making a positive precedents time line. Go back over your life and bring to mind your successes, your growth spurts, and your victories. List them. Stick with events you remember, not those that you were told. How far back you're able to go isn't important. The abridged time line of a fifty-year-old woman might include the following: "Age 4: wrote name. Age 7: rode two-wheeler. Age 12: sang solo at school assembly. Age 17: won scholarship. Age 28: stopped drinking. Age 31: son born. Age 42: master's degree. Age 50: silver wedding anniversary."

A positive precedents time line is visual evidence of both your capabilities and life's generosity. It's human nature to focus on the ways we've fallen short and extrapolate from these evidence for continued failure. Realizing that we have set some extremely positive precedents is solid backing for thinking well of the future.

Look for the good—in yourself and all around you. Positive thinking may not be a panacea, but it is the most basic way we have to cooperate with benevolence.

50.

KEEP A JOURNAL

The key to a journal's effectiveness is that you simply put pen to paper and see what you get.

One of the most direct means for contacting the psyche is with a pen and paper. Writing helps you see through confusion and bring challenges down to conquerable size. It is an invaluable aid in creating a charmed life.

You can write in your journal on your best days, when you want to record for posterity how brilliant and amazing you are. And you can write in your journal on the days when you're wrestling with a decision; when you can't concentrate; or when you're in the doldrums without a clear reason for being there and you can't even blame it on PMS. During those times when it's hard to talk to another person, or even make sense of what you're feeling yourself, a journal can be a great friend.

Your journal has two primary functions: one is to create a diary; the other is to clear out mental and emotional cobwebs. In its diary aspect, it can keep track of your life. Diaries are egocentric and mundane. That's fine. They're not for public consumption. Example: "August 24. I went out for breakfast. When I asked for the check, the waiter said an 'anonymous good Samaritan' had paid for everybody in nonsmoking. Wow! I tipped double." Stuff and nonsense. Pleasures and memories. Documentation of your days.

The journal's loftier function is in helping you sort through tangled feelings, work through dilemmas, and tap into inner resources that can be impeded when you're racking your brain to figure something out. Getting your emotions down on paper can clear the blockages that impede creativity. It can also keep you from losing your temper or sinking into self-pity.

The key to a journal's effectiveness is that you simply put pen to paper and see what you get. You don't have to be a writer. In fact, journaling can be hardest for writers, since we always want to sound good. That kind of agenda interferes with an unfettered flow of ideas from the unconscious. Another name for the journaling process is "free writing." It only works if you do it freely and without expectations.

Don't make writing in a journal one of those obligations you feel guilty about every time you don't do it. Some women thrive on daily journaling, even if it's only to say, "November 19: I don't have anything to write about." Others write intermittently and benefit each time. I'm in their camp. I keep my journal in my nightstand next to the flashlight and use it for the same reason: extra light.

Women who are enthusiastic about their journals take the low-tech route more often than not. They write with a smooth-flowing pen in a lined notebook. You certainly can do journal writing on a computer or in one of those lovely, clothbound blank books, but when you write in a 99¢ spiral notebook you're more likely to do what you're supposed to: just write. When people get fancier, they tend to worry about spelling, punctuation, and margins, which, in this context, don't matter one whit.

Some women dismiss journaling altogether because they fear someone could find their notebook, read it, and cause no end of distress. Several years ago, I left my journal in an Arby's. I was horrified to think that the young workers there had passed around my innermost thoughts like an illicit copy of *Playboy*. I realize now that my life at the time was not nearly interesting enough to merit that level of attention.

But people reluctant to keep a journal generally aren't worried about strangers as much as about the people they live with. Like sealed mail, a journal is supposed to be private and sacrosanct, and everyone in the household needs to have this awareness. It's foolish to keep a journal out in the open to tempt curiosity, but you shouldn't have to worry about someone snooping, either. If you write something intensely personal or something that could hurt someone else if read, simply destroy those pages. You don't have to save everything you write. The benefit is in the process. The evidence is in your life.

51.

MAKE THE BED

There are a variety of basic disciplines that can help you feel efficient, organized, and capable.

Because there are so many circumstances over which we have no control, it is liberating to consciously take control of those we can do something about. That's why making the bed every morning can be such an important habit.

It's something you can do shortly after you awaken, so, most of the time, you can perform this lovely little ritual before any calamities have taken place. It symbolically gives closure to the previous twenty-four hours, opening your way into an unsullied day. Since the bed is probably the largest piece of furniture in the room, making it presents a picture of order. If you're home during the day, just looking in that room can give you a feeling of calm and accomplishment. If you're away, remembering that your bed is made can help you feel efficient, organized, and capable.

There are a variety of basic disciplines in addition to making the bed that can put you in this state of mind. If I tried to do all of these all the time, I'd be crazy. Doing some of them most of the time keeps me sane. Use as a starting point this list of suggestions from women with charmed lives (and charmed lives in the making). Then let it spark ideas of your own.

Have clean hair every day.

Sit down for as many meals as possible (see Secret 21, "Drink Good Coffee, Eat Good Food").

Floss.

Sort the mail into answer, pay, and file stacks, and discard the rest.

Read (or tell) the kids a bedtime story—even by phone if you have to be away.

Drink a daily glass of freshly made carrot juice.

Empty clutter out of the car every evening.

Get out clothes for work the night before.

Brush the dog.

Provide a monthly lingerie budget so there's nothing threadbare in the drawers.

Allow no dirty dish to exist outside the dishwasher or a sinkful of sudsy water.

Reserve the last half-hour of the workday for clearing off your desk and tending to meddlesome details—it makes mornings a lot more pleasant.

Balance the checkbook within three days of receiving the statement.

Put candles on the table at dinner.

Exercise regularly.

Defy gravity by keeping clothes picked up and hung up.

Have a reliable midday phone chat with your own true love.

Write in a journal (see Secret 50, "Keep a Journal").

Recycle all cans, bottles, and paper.

Be sure you've helped somebody. This one, like making the bed, is best done every day.

52.

PREVENT PREDICTABLE
ANNOYANCES

*There's no way to completely eliminate petty annoyances,
but you can cut back on the ones that happen
over and over.*

"No one ever tripped over Pike's Peak," my friend Mary Beth used to tell me. "It's the little stuff that gets you." She was right. When a serious problem arises, we mobilize our defenses. The body pumps adrenaline and the mind taps its wisdom reserves. In times of crisis, family and friends come through, and doctors, lawyers, clergy, and counselors are in their glory. For the daily harassments, though, you're usually on your own.

How many times do you find yourself saying, "It's no big deal," with your teeth clenched and your temperature rising? A collection of "no big deals" can turn an otherwise decent day into a very big deal. Such aggravations also demand attention that could be going toward creating the life you were meant to live.

Here's a morning full of typical—preventable—"no big deals": Somebody didn't set the alarm clock, so you get a late start. (It's no big deal—just ten minutes.) The cap was left off the toothpaste and it's grown a disgusting little toothpaste callous. (No big deal. Wash off the brush and start over.) The coffee scoop is missing and you brew something that tastes as if it could cure the plague. (No big deal. There's coffee at work.) That loose button flies off your coat and down the heat vent. (No big deal. There's a spare in the sewing box upstairs.) You miss the bus. (No big deal. They run every seven minutes. Of course, you're already ten minutes late.)

You get the picture. It's nice to be serene, but a saint would be on edge after a morning like that. There's no way to completely eliminate petty annoyances, but you can cut back on the ones that happen over and over. What makes you repeatedly frantic? Make a list of these besetments and deal with each one with the same focus you would have for a project at the office.

Take keys, for instance, a common bête noir. They're easy to lose, hard to find, and possible to leave in automobile ignitions, sometimes with the motor running. If you have more control over your adult children than you do over your keys, brainstorm foolproof solutions. You might install a key rack inside every entrance door, hide house and car keys in a safe spot outside, give keys to a couple of trustworthy friends so somebody can always get into your house and car, go to a lock shop and get one of those plastic pouches for carrying a couple of critical keys in your wallet, and if you've been known to impound both your keys and your purse in the car, join a motor club with a liberal lock-out policy.

It may sound like overkill, but once such an anti-annoyance system is in place, it's an unobtrusive way to have more time and feel more peace. Defusing potential irritations makes more sense than fighting full-blown ones. When you do, small problems won't seem so overwhelming because you'll immediately shift into solutions mode. You'll become one of those people who fixes what's broken, cleans what's dirty, picks up what's on the floor, and takes care of what needs doing before situations become critical. My mother used to tell me, "A stitch in time saves nine." It still does.

53.

BE TRUE TO YOURSELF

*Life has planted within us a reliable gauge for measuring
our proximity to our true selves: when we get too
far away, we feel rotten.*

Shakespeare could turn advice into poetry: "This above all else, to thine own self be true. And it will follow as the night the day, thou canst not then be false to any man."

When the beliefs, values, and opinions of people around you and the culture at large bombard from all sides, digging out what is really "thine own self" can take a pickax and shovel. Luckily, life has planted within us a reliable gauge for measuring our proximity to our true selves: when we get too far away, we feel rotten.

A while back, I was asked to take the volunteer post of newsletter editor for a professional organization. I declined, citing my deadline on this book. The president was sympathetic and asked if I would be willing to be editor in name only until the book was done. It still didn't feel right, but I had no backup excuse and reluctantly agreed. After all, I figured, I've got a six-month reprieve. (So why was I feeling like I'd just bought a time-share in New Guinea because the salesman said, "No payments for six months"?)

Within a week, I learned that although I wasn't yet in charge of the newsletter, I was expected at a dinner Friday night and a board meeting Saturday afternoon. Looking around the table after Friday's meal, I saw women I admired. At some future point, I would edit the White Pages just to get to spend time with them. But I was also feeling sick to my stomach, and it wasn't from the food.

With a classic "gut reaction," my body knew before my brain did that in taking this on I could not be true to myself. Some months before, after ten years as a single mom, I had remarried, thereby rearranging the world of my teenage daughter and inviting into my life a wonderful man and, part of the time, his three children. Dividing my physical and emotional resources among them, a large house, and a demanding dual career as an author and speaker barely yielded a positive net. To jump into a new obligation would be, in a word, nuts.

At the meeting the next day, I resigned before being formally voted in. As I was clearly in the wrong for taking so long to know my own mind, this felt like sending my ego in for a root canal. Nevertheless, my stomach was content and so was I.

There are accepted rules for everything from using grammar to playing Monopoly, but there are no rules for being true to yourself, because only you know how to do it. With sufficient practice, it doesn't have to take waiting until the eleventh hour and making a fool of yourself.

What are you doing in your life now that you know without question is right for you? This is a tougher inquiry than it sounds. Your answers may not all seem lofty, and they may not harmonize with each other like voices in a well-trained choir. "Buying only designer clothing" could be next to "feeding the homeless" on your list. Don't worry about it. This is not a race to sainthood. It's a way to get to know yourself better.

And not every answer you give has to be a nonstop joy. Working at your job may be there, even if it's boring, repetitive, and doesn't use your education or your best skills. If that job is supporting your children or making possible the next step on your life path, you're being true to yourself every time you file another paper or solder another component to a circuit board.

Your charmed life is uniquely yours. It will grow out of being true to your earnest yearnings and your most sacred commitments. To the vast majority of people, those living by what they think others expect of them, you may at times appear selfish, ungrateful, antisocial, and like the proverbial stick-in-the-mud. From those also being true to themselves, expect empathy and respect.

54.

INSTALL NECESSARY UPGRADES

You can start your upgrade process with the simplest of discernments, choosing something that's just a bit delightful over something that isn't.

It is extraordinary, when you think about it, how well just about everybody does. A remarkable majority of us have homes, jobs, and people to love. Some of our fellow humans, however, have it even better. Their lives sparkle. If the rest of us are eating cake, theirs has frosting.

Like nearly everybody else, these men and women come into the world with sufficient intelligence, common sense, and resources to get by. This is like the basic software package you get when you buy a new computer. "Basic" means it can do many things adequately and few optimally. Therefore, most people purchase an upgraded version. When it comes to living, however, only an adept minority think to install an upgrade. They refuse to settle for a four-font existence.

You can upgrade every aspect of your life without a lot of money and with no more time than you're spending now. Essential elements of upgraded living include these: Unique is usually better than commonplace. Handmade is usually better than mass-produced. Beautiful is usually better than ugly and always better than neutral. Engaging beats dull, hands down.

You can start your upgrade process with the simplest of discernments, choosing something that's just a bit delightful over something that isn't. For example:

Toothpaste. What kind of toothpaste do you use? Is it the same mint stuff your mother bought for you? Think of the tiny tingle you'll experience every morning if you select a more interesting variety. Natural-food stores have a dazzling array of them: orange and strawberry, cinnamon and myrrh, herbal toothpaste from India and homeopathic toothpaste from Germany. Any day that begins with imported toothpaste has got to have some terrific moments in it.

Greeting cards. For the same two or three dollars you'd spend on an ordinary card that's read and tossed, you can pick up a little work of art the recipient might tuck away in a steamer trunk for her great-great-grandchildren to discover. Don't limit yourself to the supermarket or the pharmacy: buy cards from art museums, specialty booksellers, and antique shops, and save them for the proper occasion. When you send one, put in a photograph, a bookmark, an embroidered handkerchief, a piece of fruit leather, or a sheet of stickers. (You could really shock somebody and put in a five-dollar bill. Why do we think it's okay to surprise a child in this way but not an adult?)

Vegetables. It's easy to fall into the corn, peas, and iceberg lettuce rut. Rethink the vegetable kingdom! Serve a salad of tangy baby greens (they come already washed and ready). Have yams instead of white potatoes, even when it isn't Thanksgiving (they're far more nutritious, and they're orange). When my husband's children came to stay the first time after our marriage, I knew the wrong vegetable could put me in evil stepmother category in short order. I fixed artichokes and put an empty stainless steel bowl in the center of the table for tossing the leaves. It's quite a vegetable that can make throwing food okay.

These are little things, but life is a collection of little things. In a charmed life, there's simply some thought behind them. Upgrade some aspect of your life today. Upgrade another tomorrow or next week. It's necessary.

55.

BOOST YOUR

VITALITY

*People who are genuinely healthy, who have a level of vitality
that sets them apart from the lethargic masses, feel so
good they think they're living charmed lives no matter what
else is going on.*

Frail and wan are fine for the fainting maidens in old poems and
operatic divas in the final act, but they're major stumbling blocks
to creating a charmed life. People who are genuinely healthy, who
have a level of vitality that sets them apart from the lethargic
masses, feel so good that they think they're living charmed lives
no matter what else is going on.

Invest in vitality by giving your physical well-being a high priority. We all know the boring basics, "eat right and exercise." It
sounds like a prison term: twenty years, broccoli and the treadmill, no parole. Taking care of your health has to become more of
an adventure and less of a chore or only the unusually motivated
will stay with it.

The adventure begins when you involve your whole being in
the *idea* of being healthy. This doesn't take any time, since it's
simply a matter of substituting one way of thinking for another.
See yourself as healthy, regardless of appearances or history. A
wise teacher shared with me years ago that I had to first make up

my mind to be healthy. The rest would follow naturally because, as he put it, "Healthy people do healthy things." To be a genuinely healthy person, do these things:

Speak well of your physical self. Use words such as *robust, hearty, strong, vibrant, fit,* and *vigorous* in referring to yourself—both in conversation with others and in the conversations inside your head. Get rid of words like *weak, susceptible, fatigued,* and *fat.* If you've gained some weight, refer to it as a writer friend of mine did: "I've enhanced my body." You're then free to shed the enhancement or keep it, but you don't have to hate yourself either way.

Eat food that's fresh and alive. If you spend more time in the middle aisles of the supermarket than at the edges where the fresh food is, you're cheating yourself. Enjoy all the fresh fruits and vegetables you can get your hands on—raw, juiced, or lightly steamed. Get excited over a plump peach or a perfect persimmon. If you can grow a garden or go to a farmer's market for produce picked just hours before, do it. Your food can't give you any more life than it has itself.

Challenge yourself physically. This doesn't have to mean cliff climbing or rafting through rapids, but it might mean roller-skating with your kids or meeting a friend for a walk instead of a doughnut. Respect your limitations and use good sense, but don't let yourself get decrepit before your time. Remember the old saw that more people rust out than wear out.

Take a drug test. No, not one of those drug tests—I'm referring to looking at your lifestyle to see how many pharmaceuticals you ingest on a regular basis. If you take prescription medications prescribed by more than one doctor, have you checked with a pharmacist to see that they're all compatible? Do you take over-the-counter medicines? Could you take fewer of them by substituting natural alternatives or by making minor lifestyle alterations? Do you smoke? Do you drink alcohol? (Even moderate alcohol consumption has been linked with breast cancer.) How much caffeine do you take in through coffee, strong tea, and cola? How does it affect you?

Associate with healthy people. Even adults are subject to a certain amount of peer pressure. Make it the positive sort by being around people whose lifestyles you wish to emulate.

Become easygoing. If it's not your nature, pretend. Your blood pressure won't know you're faking. Physical activity, being around natural or artistic beauty, mental/physical disciplines like yoga and tai chi, meditation (see Secret 5, "Take Ten"), and faith in a higher power are great stress reducers. So is having a cat, or a grandchild.

56.

SANCTIFY THE ORDINARY

*Redefine "spiritual life" so that it's your day-to-day life,
lived well, with intention, integrity, and well-placed awe.
Eating a meal, resolving a conflict, scraping the ice off
your windshield some morning in January—all these
can be spiritual practice.*

Creating a charmed life is a spiritual undertaking because its impetus comes from the deepest part of us. Traditionally, religion was like lingerie: men controlled the business, but women were the primary consumers. This is not because women were inherently holier—or needier—than men. It was because the lives we led as women directed us to construct spiritual lives from the stuff of everyday experience. Our physiology connected us with the rhythms of nature, and our historic relegation to a limited role in society caused us to grow souls before we could grow corporations.

The fact that we are now "out in the world" has not lessened this proclivity. It has, in fact, expanded it. The "woman's touch" that once meant only curtains at the windows or a bouquet on the table has become a humanizing influence in business, politics, and religious institutions.

But while we collectively alter the culture, we individually run the risk of a diminished connection with our inner richness. The vast majority of us are tired, overscheduled, and have stuck too many of our dreams in the middle desk drawer beneath the rubber bands, last month's bank statement, and half a bottle of Tylenol. Far too many women are suffering from a chronic loss of wonder.

Some remedy this with spiritual disciplines of various kinds, but those who most need what these disciplines promise can't find the time to devote to them. The only viable alternative is to turn the business of living into a spiritual exercise.

To do this, it is necessary to transfer spirituality from *out there* to *around here*. Redefine "spiritual life" so that it's your day-to-day life, lived well, with intention, integrity, and well-placed awe. Eating a meal, resolving a conflict, scraping the ice off your windshield some morning in January—all these can be spiritual practice. And if you scrape the ice off your husband's windshield, too, you might get a glimpse of nirvana.

This attitude, this paying acute attention to the happenings of your day, the Buddhists call *mindfulness*. When you're mindful, even during hectic times, none of this twenty-four-hour gift gets away from you. St. Paul's advice to "pray without ceasing" is similar. It's possible to make a prayer or an offering of every experience when you view each one, aggravations included, as an episode in a larger story.

If you're the pragmatic sort, this may be a daunting leap. Remember that although regarding life as a spiritual adventure may be a new concept to your rational mind, it's an ancient truth to your very being as a woman. Stored within your cells, each one constructed of recycled atoms as old as the earth, is the timeless truth women have always known: all life is sacred, seamless, endless, connected.

As you allow the events of your day to take on spiritual significance, you'll notice more happy coincidences coming into play. You'll find yourself becoming more insightful. You will catch your breath a little more often when you spot some natural wonder like a magnificent sunset or your magnificent dog. You'll more often feel content in the present and trusting of the future. Even for those of us who cut our teeth on the belief that we could "have it all," having all this is usually enough.

57.

CHECK IN:

ARE YOU BEING SERVED?

When you've detoured a few yards to get yourself taken care of, you'll be able to go the extra mile in caring for others with far less likelihood of resentment or regret.

Sometimes you just want somebody to pump your gas. Or wash your hair. Or bring you dinner. This desire doesn't come from being lazy or incapable. It arises out of the immutable law of balance: You're serving people all the time. If somebody doesn't serve you back, the balance is lost. Balance is essential not only for a charmed life but for life itself. Scientists call this *homeostasis*. When the balance is upset in nature, there's ecological disruption. When the balance goes off in the body, disease results. When the balance is off-kilter in our lives, we end up uncomfortable, even bitter.

It was traditionally believed—by half the population at least—that women could derive sufficient satisfaction from serving others. The pendulum swung in the latter part of the twentieth century to looking out for number one, to putting achievement for ourselves ahead of attachment to others. Each extreme gave us some fulfillment, but always with the nagging thought that we were missing something important. We were.

Today, most women are trying to do right by everybody. We give the mythical 110 percent to our families, our jobs, and (we like to think) ourselves. Our motivation is excellent. However, as my grandmother used to say, "The spirit is willing, but the flesh is weak." Bound as we are by laws of physics and physiology, we don't have 110 percent to give, much less 330. One way to balance our lives, to give what we need to give and keep what we need to keep, is to allow others to serve us a little bit every day.

At a meeting of women writers a while back, Deborah caught everyone's attention by saying that her relationship with Ron, her significant other, had become "interesting." We all leaned in closer so we wouldn't miss anything good. "I'm seeing what a really wonderful thing this is," Deborah went on. "Last week, Ron did my laundry." (There was a collective gasp.) "And he folded it." (Sighs.) "No one ever did my laundry before."

On that suburban townhouse patio sat a dozen accomplished women in our thirties, forties, and fifties, each one thriving in the highly competitive business of freelance writing. All of us are currently or formerly married. We're well traveled, well educated, and reasonably sophisticated. But when Deborah told us that her intended had actually *folded* her laundry, we were reduced to the incoherent babbling of infatuated adolescents. Why? We hadn't been allowing ourselves to be served enough.

Getting served is no easy matter in this day of self-service everything. You have to look for ways to get your service needs met and not let anyone tell you you're being a prima donna for doing it.

If you despise filing and organizing, for instance, there are people who do that sort of thing for a reasonable fee. Would you love to have a cleaning person? Check the ads and bulletin boards.

Having someone in to help even once a month can keep housework from overwhelming you. If you want to be pampered, take a day off for one of those spa extravaganzas—facial, manicure, pedicure, seaweed wrap (what the heck, it comes with it), haircut, and the rest. If the cost is prohibitive, get a comparable experience in luxury at a beauty school for a pittance.

Be discerning: only you know how you would really appreciate being served and what would just seem silly. I personally like getting my gas at Murphy's Service (what a concept) Station where there are no self-service pumps, and they always wash the windows and check the oil and tire pressure.

I'm also a great fan of massage. Getting one every week would take more money than I'm willing to part with, but one every three weeks doesn't, and I've read that the immune-system benefits of a good massage last twenty-one days.

I even call the personal shopper at an elegant specialty store every year or so when I'm ready for my Major Suit Purchase. It doesn't matter that I have a frequent-buyer card at the Junior League Thrift Store: once a year I get to luxuriate in an elegant sitting room behind a trompe l'oeil door, drink imported water from midnight-blue stemware, and have somebody else do up my zipper.

Whatever minor indulgences you choose, their payoff is more energy, both physical and emotional. When you've detoured a few yards to get yourself taken care of, you'll be able to go the extra mile in caring for others with far less likelihood of resentment or regret.

58.

DIG IN
THE DIRT

When you want to create a rich, satisfying life and much of your time is already accounted for, it's important to focus on endeavors that do double-duty. Gardening, if it appeals to you, is one of those.

Not everyone who lives a charmed life is a gardener, but enough are that it's worth considering. Tending greenery, flowers, and vegetables is an "omega experience": an activity that takes place in that amazing realm where matter and spirit meet. Digging in the dirt, getting close to the creepers and crawlers that live there, and feeding the soil with cow manure is pretty earthy stuff. And yet the life that somehow enters in to push a plant up through the ground goes beyond material explanation.

When you want to create a rich, satisfying life and much of your time is already accounted for, it's important to focus on endeavors that do double-duty. Gardening, if it appeals to you, is one of those. Even if your gardening is confined to a window box or apartment balcony, it can soften the edges of a rough day. It's a way to get some necessary alone time and, if you love it, it can put you in the same state of peace you'd reach by sitting in formal meditation. It provides exercise, as well as a way to get fresh air and sunshine. (Avoiding the midday sun is prudent, of course, but we need some sun in the morning or late afternoon, both for vitamin D and emotional uplift.)

If you have children and they like to be involved with growing things—little ones almost always do—gardening can be quality time spent with them. It also gives children more of a feel for nature than any book about nature, as well as one more tool for creating charmed lives of their own.

Working outside with your true love can be a bonding experience as well, or, if gardening is not for you, appreciating your partner's efforts can provide you with some of the benefits vicariously. It was my husband, a far greater connoisseur of peat moss and compost than I, who came up with these "Ten Steps to a Spiritual Outdoors":

1. Be sure your garden reflects your personality and your family's. If it makes you feel calm and reflective, safe and comfortable, then your garden is a reflection of you.

2. Make it simple and easy to maintain. Tend toward simple structures. Emphasize low-maintenance plants and perennials. Don't extend a workaholic lifestyle into your garden.

3. Use what you have been given by nature and history. Work with existing trees and bushes. A rock pile can become a rock garden, an old clothesline pole a trellis for a climbing rose.

4. Avoid an assembly-line garden through personal touches with private meaning. You might bury a secret love letter to be opened on some future anniversary. Use your imagination to make your garden personally yours.

5. Remember the rules of common-sense gardening. Know the soil, sun, and nutrient needs of your plants. It is not good gardening to plant something doomed to struggle or die.

6. Bring your garden into your home. Plant herbs near the kitchen door or in pots on a sunny windowsill. Many vegetables can be effectively interspersed with ornamental plants. Decorate your home and your office with your own cut flowers.

7. Provide for nature with your landscaping. Make it friendly to birds and small animals, and avoid garden products that are harmful to them. If you're willing to keep them maintained, install bird baths and feeders.

8. For everybody's sake, use natural garden products and methods when you can. There are ways to protect your garden without endangering the surrounding environment (which happens to be your environment).

9. Don't fight irrefutable truths. If you have a dog, an attractive run of bark mulch along the fence will make for less stress—on you and the dog—than delicate plantings. If you have children who need play space, give it to them. An open area with base paths worn in the grass can be as beautiful as a summer garden when it's filled with laughing children.

10. Consider your garden a family affair. Set aside a special bed for each family member. Don't expect children's plots to look the way yours would. Childhood, like blossoms, is fleeting. Enjoy both while you can.

59.

WHEN HEAVEN KNOCKS, OPEN THE DOOR

Scan your memory and bring to mind at least one time when you were privy to some inexplicable wonder.

When I was a teenager and believed that all things were not only possible but likely, I wrote to my pen pal Linda Adler that I wanted to be a mystic when I grew up. I longed to have the life-changing awakening that connected people like Whitman and Wordsworth and Blake with Martin Buber, Teresa of Avila, and Saul on the road to Damascus. I wanted to encounter the ultimate ecstasy of knowing without question that every expression of life is interwoven with every other, and that I am an integral part of this grand festival. Linda suggested that I start by becoming a "progressive lady theologian," since one could at least study for that in college.

During the intervening years, I thought I knew only one person who had had a bona fide mystical experience. It happened to my first husband's sister Rita. When she was visiting in India, she lay down for a mid-morning rest and was instead lifted from her body and her standard awareness to a consciousness that could only be described as cosmic. She reported feeling the vastness of impersonal and unconditional love and the certainty that even the most painful earthly experience is ultimately for good.

She said that she learned without any doubt that we are somehow simultaneously both dust and divine, and that there is a state of mind in which such a notion is not even perplexing.

I was awestruck by her story—and at first a little jealous. After all, she'd gotten what I'd wanted since my Clearasil days. Now I might be subject to some heavenly nepotism clause: only one mystic per family.

In ruminating over Rita's incident, though, I began to realize that every woman I know, myself included, has had transcendent experiences. Amazing things happen—around the death of a loved one or the birth of a child, in the early-morning quiet or some place of great natural beauty, or even in a spot as unlikely as a rush-hour subway. At these times, every so often, when we're not expecting anything other than our next breath, we touch something beyond ourselves.

This doesn't have to be an otherworldly event like a near-death experience or having an angel show up at the foot of the bed. It can be running into a stranger who might as well be an angel because he or she tells you precisely what you need to hear. It can happen in the midst of a crisis that has no apparent solution, when you suddenly know as well as you know your name that everything will work out. You might glimpse it when you find yourself acting with more courage or love or selflessness than you thought you had in you.

These magic moments sprinkle stardust on our lives. We tend to take them for granted, though, going back to our narrower focus as if the heavens had not just opened to give us a peek.

Scan your memory, if you haven't already, and bring to mind

at least one time when you were privy to some inexplicable wonder. Whether you think of it often or not, whether or not you've discussed it with other people, or even if you tried to discuss it and were met with ridicule or indifference, you received a priceless gift. It was designed for you and inscribed to you.

Learning from what others believe to be true can bring beauty to your life, just as ready-to-wear clothing can bring beauty to your closet. But the truth you've touched for yourself is custom-tailored—created to fit you and bring out your best. This is truth you can use in your life without amendment or translation.

Divinity communicates in many ways: coincidence, inspiration, dreams, books, films, people, nature, art, hunches. Look for your brushes with the divine. Be receptive to them. When heaven knocks, open the door. Value these visits. Remember them. Expect more of them.

60.

BAN THE BUZZ

Although we depend on the electronic accoutrements of modern life, our cells and our souls need something else. Indulge them, part of the time at least, in a charmed environment that's free of beeps, bleeps, and buzzes.

The refrigerator whirs, the dishwasher chugs, the computer hums, a video game blips, and the spin cycle very nearly roars. For most of us it's a rare day that we get to hear unadulterated silence, or at least the clean sounds of nature without an electronic echo.

A lot of irritability can be traced to the aural assault to which we're constantly subject. It's well established that certain kinds of music, as well as natural sounds like flowing water or a crackling fire, calm people down. Conversely, sounds like the proverbial chalk on a blackboard can make your skin crawl.

Scientists who study gender differences have found that, generally speaking, woman are more sensitive to sounds than men are, probably because mothers through the ages have learned to be alert to their babies' cries and whimpers. This heightened sensitivity can be useful, but it's a vexation in an age when so many of the sounds we hear are artificial and annoying.

Although we depend on the electronic accoutrements of modern life, our cells and our souls need something else. Indulge them, part of the time at least, in a charmed environment that's free of beeps, bleeps, and buzzes. For example:

Turn off machinery when you're not using it.

Look for quieter alternatives to noisy gadgets. Comparison shop for noise levels when you're in the market for home appliances or office equipment.

Unplug! Does your can opener or citrus juicer really have to be automatic? If you look for them, you can find manual versions of many things we're used to seeing motorized.

When you're going a short distance, walk or ride your bike.

Sit in a park and listen to the birds.

Fix faucets that drip, toilets that run, and other reparable noisemakers.

Choose a restaurant that doesn't believe you have to get the Top 40 with your lunch.

Watch TV if your want to, but don't use it as a backdrop for life. Never let a television entertain an empty room.

Treat your ears to your favorite music, live when possible. Play the piano, go to a chamber music concert, see some stirring musical theater, or invite over a couple of friends who will bring guitars.

Invest in an indoor fountain. It's like having a babbling brook in your living room any time you want one. Also, because these little joys are themselves plug-in devices, they provide a reminder that problems often carry their own solutions.

61.

WELCOME YOURSELF HOME

This is your home we're talking about: a place so sacred, so private, and so yours that you need a key to get into it.

Home used to be where a woman could be kept in her assigned place. The backlash to that was an almost wholesale abandonment of home and hearth in favor of a time clock and a paycheck. Now *balance* is the buzzword, but for most of us that equilibrium is precarious.

Through speaking on my book about home, *Shelter for the Spirit*, I've met hundreds of women who have shared with me their internal battles with domesticity. Those who work full-time often feel overwhelmed, and, if they have children, they often feel guilty. Those who don't work for pay frequently find themselves on the defensive, as if they had to single-handedly convince an entire culture that raising the next generation is a job worth doing.

Whatever her individual circumstances, nobody I've talked with can figure out how to transform herself into the media ideal: queen of a corporate empire, but able to find time to spawn sourdough culture, tend fledgling petunias, and create awesome centerpieces with nothing but dried weeds and a glue gun. This is not because of any lack of ingenuity on the part of women; it's because sculpting our lives into media-prescribed proportions is about as realistic as sculpting our bodies into Barbie proportions.

Nevertheless, everyone who has ever created a charmed life has found balance between her life at home and her contributions to the larger world. These people have also loved their homes and found genuine refreshment there. It is critical to remember that *home* is not a synonym for *house* or *apartment*. Home is a place to rest and recreate both body and soul. Like home plate in baseball, it's the place where you can stop running.

For too many people, coming home is like arriving at a second job. With all the chores to do, bills to pay, mail to answer, e-mail to answer, and the rest, home can seem more like a pit stop than a sanctuary. It's essential to see that if living a charmed life were an art, your home would be your studio. If it were a science, your home would be your laboratory.

Bring some domestic bliss—or at least a greater degree of domestic tranquillity—into your home and your life by realizing:

Your home is 1 percent structure and contents, 99 percent living beings. Home is yourself, the people you live with, your pets, and your plants. The contentment of the living beings in a house or apartment is far and away its most salient factor.

Your home needs to be a reflection of yourself, not of your decorator or a design magazine. If you're going to judge the way it looks, ask, "Does my home look like me?" or, if you have a family, "Does our home look like us?"

Home is the place where you are most thoroughly yourself, with no pretenses. It is the place where you feel most intensely and grow most prolifically. Seemingly thankless home-maintenance chores can be surprising teachers of humility, patience, and acceptance.

Balance between home and work, family and friends, interior pursuits and exterior endeavors is extremely personal. There are plenty of self-styled experts who like to pontificate for the rest of us, but only you know what you need in order to feel in tune, enthusiastic, and at peace.

We hear so many conflicting messages about what we're supposed to do and be that it's easy to tune into one of those voices and decide it's ours. But this is your home we're talking about: a place so sacred, so private, and so *yours* that you need a key to get into it. It's the last place you want people who don't even know you, much less love you, deciding how you should conduct your life.

Listen to yourself. Trust yourself. Apply your own conclusions to helping the place where you live better serve your soul, your family, and your dreams.

62.

CALL A TRUCE WITH
THE CLOCK

*You have a function on this planet. There may not be time
to have a clean house, a clean car, and clean hair all on
the same day, but there is time to do what you came
here for—and fit in a little sightseeing.*

When I was in eighth grade, Joy Baer was in my gym class. She carried a Bible and always wore skirts that covered her knees. I thought she went a little far with the goody-goody thing. But there was something intriguing about Joy Baer: she was the only girl in eighth grade phys ed who never rushed to get ready for her next class. "The Lord held the sun for Joshua," she told me once. "I figure He'll hold the bell for me."

I can't say that God Almighty ever affected the operation of the school bell at Westport Junior High, but Joy never worried about being late, and she never was. She somehow knew that there was plenty of time, even though she had the same five minutes between classes as the rest of us. I have since learned that she was right. There *is* plenty of time, and when you act on this assumption, time stretches—not just for Joy and Joshua, but for anybody.

Our relationship with time is, in part, subjective. We say "The time flew by" and also, "Time stood still." Along with giving it wings and feet, we give time tremendous power. Time intimidates us because we realize it is the true currency of a lifetime, and nobody knows how to create more of it. Joy Baer did a pretty good job, though, and she was only thirteen. Like her, you can take simple steps to help stretch your time:

Decide you have time for what's important. This includes rest, leisure, and do-nothing time. Once you make that decision, you'll chart your days differently. You'll say no to the extraneous. You won't let a long-winded stranger, friend, or salesperson steal time from you.

Do the important thing first. Whether it's working on your novel or taking your kids to the park, do what matters to you first—even if there are dishes in the sink and messages on the answering machine. If you claim even half an hour to do what you really, really want, your time will start to seem like pants with an elastic waist: roomy and accommodating. You will somehow get around to the dishes, but without giving it priority attention, you might never have gotten around to your novel.

Get comfortable with empty time. Some people panic when every minute isn't planned out and filled up. Even being early for a movie makes them nervous. That's because in empty time we have to be with ourselves and our thoughts. When you stop saturating every second of open time with activity, you'll realize that there really is more time than you thought. Use some of it to sit, breathe, and regroup.

Be willing *to do less.* A mentor once said to me, "Stop doing so damn much stuff to make yourself feel important." Yikes! But she was right: I'd put myself on an invisible treadmill to prove my value. None of us has to justify her existence. See what eats up your time and lessen that, get rid of it, or delegate it. Are you addicted to busywork because your real work is too scary to tackle? Are you on the phone too much? Does perfectionism at home or at the office keep you busy all the time? Be willing to do less and see what happens to your relationship with time.

Stop saying things like "There aren't enough hours in the day" and "I just never have time anymore." Using these phrases can be a way to fish for compliments or sympathy. You might get both, but at a price. Your unconscious latches onto statements like this and works to turn your words into your reality. If you want to talk about time, quote physicist Erwin Schroedinger: "The present is the only thing that has no end."

Use clocks with hands. Futurist Jeremy Rifkin has commented that the prevalence of digital clocks and watches separates us from time as a continuum. We see that it is 10:17. What can be achieved at 10:17? Practically nothing. But seeing an actual minute hand between the 3 and the 4 gives you the image of time as a circle. The work you did in the past is creating your life in the present. There *is* time.

Remember what you're here for. If you're religious enough to feel that you're here to do God's will, you can know that God is going to support that intention with adequate time. If you're not religious, think about your purpose or your calling. You have a function on this planet. There may not be time to have a clean house, a clean car, and clean hair all on the same day, but there is time to do what you came here for—and fit in a little sightseeing.

63.

COME UP WITH QUICK CONNECTIONS

The beauty of quick connections is that once you have a repertoire of them, you're never without a way to reroute anxiety, reconnect with yourself, and start fresh in the next moment.

Even with the best intentions, we all experience times when the serenity or flash of intuition we're after has to come *right now*—already microwaved and waiting at the drive-thru window. Quick connections, actions you can take on a moment's notice, are fast food for a charmed life, and they are more nourishing than they look. The beauty of quick connections is that once you have a repertoire of them, you're never without a way to reroute anxiety, reconnect with yourself, and start fresh in the next moment. Try some of these quick connections and add your own:

Have a childlike moment. Jump into a pile of crunchy autumn leaves. Swing in the park. Eat a jawbreaker. Blow bubbles.

Admit when you're wrong. It takes a lot of energy to rationalize a mistake, attempt to cover it up, and then feel guilty. Admitting immediately when you're wrong sets you square with the world.

Pay an honest compliment. Do this especially if you can offer a compliment to someone who is difficult for you to deal with. Identify something positive about that person and let her know.

See a picture show. This isn't going to the movies: it's providing yourself with a short "picture show" of photos or drawings that make you feel good. This can be an ever-changing packet of family pictures you keep in a desk drawer, postcards of places you've been or would like to go, or images that are peaceful and serene.

Complete a task. Pick any small chore you've been putting off—writing a thank-you note, maybe, or sewing on a button. Start it and finish it. Your feeling of accomplishment will be much larger than the job that inspired it.

Smile. The simple act of smiling can make you feel less angry or frustrated. Your mind believes your face and thinks you're happy.

Pray. It's not difficult to master the skill of abbreviated prayer. It starts with the supposition that somebody is actually listening. Then you say what you need to say: "Help!" "Thanks." "Give me some insight here."

Stretch. The physical exercises of yoga were developed as preparation for meditation. People who engage in these slow, stretching motions, though, find that the exercises can be a meditation in themselves. We carry tension in our shoulders, backs, and hips. Take a minute to stretch or bend in a way that releases some of that tension.

Sweat. Researchers looked at a sizable group of yogis, lamas, and other respected teachers in India to see what, if anything, they had in common. The finding was this: all the holy men sweat for at least ten minutes a day. Even this modicum of physical exertion results in more energy and less anxiety, whether you're in India or Indiana.

Inspire yourself. Keep little books of inspiration by your bed, in the kitchen, in the bathroom, at the office. Reach for one whenever you need it. The ones on my desk right now are *Midlife Awakenings* by Barbara Bartocci, and *God Made Easy* by Patrice Karst.

Enjoy a two-minute concert. There is probably some kind of music that can make a world of difference in your world right now. Whether it's blues or bluegrass, the classics or classic rock, the music that speaks to you very likely speaks to your soul too. You don't have to retire with headphones for the afternoon; one song can do it.

Touch the earth. Walk barefoot. Repot a houseplant, or at least water one. Have a little bowl of colored stones on your desk and hold one in your hand for a bit. Think of being rooted in the earth and reaching for the heavens.

64.

REDEFINE "LADY"

*Just because current mores don't give graciousness a
high priority doesn't mean you can't.*

I recently read a news clip about a local politician who had to
publicly apologize to the women on a committee he chaired for
referring to them as "ladies." The term was, in their view,
demeaning.

I've suspected at times that I'm living in the wrong century,
but that article confirmed it. If someone wanted to insult me by
calling me a lady, I would be sufficiently out of step to take it as a
compliment. I don't think of a lady as a prefeminist throwback, a
hybrid of Melanie Wilkes and the Stepford wives. Consider two of
the women our generation has most admired: Mother Teresa,
time and again referred to as a "great lady," and the Princess of
Wales, née *Lady* Diana.

As I see it, any female past puberty is a woman. I define *lady*
as a woman of substance, refinement, and assurance—all qualities
that attract a charmed life. If you have a negative connotation of
the term, it may be because someone in your childhood told you
to "act like a lady" and really meant, "Sit still, stay quiet, and do
your best not to have an original thought." In truth, a lady most
assuredly stands up, speaks out, and thinks for herself; she just
does it in a way that makes other people feel worthwhile too.

Some time back, I attended the funeral of a former employer of mine and, like hundreds of others who knew him, I sent condolences to his family. A week later, I received in the mail notes from both his widow and his daughter, thanking me for my card and for my presence at the service. I was dumbfounded. No one expects a thank-you note for a sympathy card. That this mother and daughter sent them anyway reminded me what it means to be a lady, and how lucky I am to know some.

Joining their ranks doesn't take a grand inheritance or a life of leisure. You don't need to come out like a debutante, but rather to come into your own. Then you can esteem yourself and others enough to act with respect, courtesy, and kindness in all circumstances. Just because current mores don't give graciousness a high priority doesn't mean you can't.

The surprising secret is this: being a polite, dignified lady takes no more time or energy than being a curt, disgruntled grump. Regardless of your background, there is a lady inside you. It's not something you learn to be, but something you allow yourself to become.

As you do this, you won't necessarily change the things you do, but rather how you do them. You'll care a little bit more. You'll plan a little bit earlier. You will remember that the person looking back at you—whether the president of the company, the panhandler on the corner, or your own reflection in the mirror—is a divine idea in human dress.

Think of yourself as a lady before you answer the phone, and listen to how you sound. Think of yourself as a lady when you finally get to the checkout counter after the guy with the out-of-state check and no ID. Think of yourself as a lady on the days your boss isn't seeing herself as one. You'll be amazed at how differently you respond.

And every once in a while give yourself what my friend Suzanne calls "a lady break." You may work in construction and be raising five sons, but afternoon tea at the best hotel in town just might make your weekend. The last time Suzanne and I stole away for mini-scones, plump raspberries, and Jasmine tea in china cups, I actually wore a hat. And it wasn't even winter.

65.

MIDWIFE DREAMS

When you act as a midwife for the dreams of others, you get to watch their possibilities take shape. Subsequently, you become part of a network of people eager to assist when it's your turn to bring a new dream into being.

Never, ever, under any circumstances stomp on another person's God-given dream.

We sometimes try to help people "be realistic" by telling them what we think they couldn't possibly do. But we don't know what they can do. In my workshops, I used to tell people to dream anything within the realm of physical possibility, adding the caveat "Of course, if you're sixty years old you won't want to pursue the dream of being a dancer." Then I went to a theatrical awards ceremony featuring a tap dance troupe comprised of women in their sixties, seventies, and eighties. Now I just say, "Dream anything within the realm of physical possibility" and leave the extent of that realm open.

Supporting other people's dreams is crucial to your own charmed living, because being the only person you know who is living a charmed life would be pretty awful. You would be resented and misunderstood. When you act as a midwife for the dreams of others, you get to watch their possibilities take shape. Subsequently, you become part of a network of people eager to assist when it's your turn to bring a new dream into being.

Here are some things you can do to be instrumental in delivering dreams:

See dream nurturance as part of your role as a partner, a parent, and a friend. Conversely, cultivate relationships with those who are willing to nurture your dreams.

Encourage the dreams of those around you. Listen to these people. Believe in them. Extend expertise when you have it and practical help when you feel moved to offer it.

Help the dreamer stay on course. Dreams-come-true expert Marcia Wieder writes in her book *Doing Less and Having More*: "Ideally, you'll share [your dream] with someone who will hold you accountable, someone who will check in and ask, 'What are you doing to move that dream forward?'"

Be honest. If you're privy to a dream that you can't support, say so. Let the other person rethink her concept or find the backing she needs elsewhere. Above all, never let someone assume you're behind her dream if you're really not.

Avoid jealousy and envy. There is no limit on how many dreams can become reality. The notion "If hers comes true, maybe mine won't" is the opposite of what more often happens. I personally know ten midwives, and none of them has fewer than five children. It seems that their work so involves them with pregnancy, birth, and infants that they tend to have a lot of babies themselves. Similarly, when you act as midwife for other people's dreams, you get in the dream fulfillment business, and having your own dreams come true is all in a day's work.

66.

BUILD SOUL EQUITY

No matter what an experience looks like on the outside,
there's soul gold in there somewhere. Find it.

Everything around us has varying degrees of worth. The house you live in, for example, has a certain appraised valuation, but the replacement value given it by your insurance company is higher. And if two of your children were born there, you and your husband added on the art studio with your own labor, and your oldest daughter had her wedding there last spring, its perceived value to you is immeasurable.

Just as a realtor, an insurance adjuster, and a homeowner can place different values on a house, our ego and our soul place different values on our daily activities. It is tempting for the ego to let the boring, difficult, and unpleasant aspects of our lives convince us that life is largely boring, difficult, and unpleasant.

The soul—our animating, motivating, inner essence—can use the trials and the tedium to its benefit. It can celebrate the very circumstances that jar the ego: enduring a lengthy traffic jam or an interminable meeting, having no time to ourselves or spending too many Saturday nights alone. Living through these, and learning through them, builds soul equity that's worth more than money in the bank.

Once you're convinced that you're here to learn and grow and expand your capacity to love, know, and experience life, you'll start to value everything you do and everything that happens to you in terms of soul equity. Then you'll feel less pressure to radically alter your life or yourself. Uncovering the intangible treasures within the obligations you already have and within the woman you already are becomes much more appealing.

You build soul equity by learning the lesson within every experience, remembering it, and applying your expanded insight to a similar circumstance when it comes up later. Soul equity increases as you search out the meaning inherent in the simplest goings-on of daily life. If seeing a squirrel collecting acorns for the winter reminds you that you really ought to be saving more for your retirement, don't brush it off because you're not supposed to get investment advice from wildlife. Look for the metaphors around you, majestic truths packaged inside modest events.

From time to time, take stock of the soul equity you've capitalized to date. What did it take to acquire the patience, perseverance, wisdom, humor, and faith you have today? Whatever your process has been, you have priceless assets to show for it.

The soul equity abundant in a charmed life is not accrued only on uphill climbs. It also comes from the joys of your life, provided you're totally present to them. The paradox here is that being alert for the good things is guaranteed only when you're willing to be an equal-opportunity experiencer. You have to suit up and show up every day—whether you're taking a vacation or taking inventory, whether you have a five-year-old who's a nonstop delight or a teenager you sometimes wish would join a traveling circus.

No matter what an experience looks like on the outside, there's soul gold in there somewhere. Find it. Appreciate it. Let it figure prominently in your net worth.

67.

HONOR YOUR CYCLES

*No woman can lead a charmed life without respecting her
cyclic proclivities, both month to month and
decade to decade.*

Jesus and Buddha. Mohammed and Krishna. Abraham, Isaac, and Jacob. It makes you wonder if a necessary prerequisite for enlightenment is being one of the guys.

Historical images notwithstanding, women actually have an advantage in the soul department. As channels for creation, we're conduits for the infinite. Our cyclic patterns tie us to the oceans' tides and the phases of the moon. If we embrace our bodies' changes and rhythms instead of resenting them as biological nuisances, we can use the very act of living in these bodies to expedite our growth.

As women, we are cyclic beings. Our cycles connect us with life itself, and they have spiritual as well as physical ramifications. If we understand our cyclic nature, we can see how some of its stages stimulate our outgoing side, while others encourage more inward propensities. Together they help mold us into a more balanced and more fully evolved whole.

When my daughter reached the age of learning about the menstruation process, I was immersed in the writings of Tamara Slayton, an inspired educator on the inner side of feminine cycles. Brimming with new knowledge to share, I told Rachael that women honor their femininity by being aware of the emotional subtleties of their cycle—becoming more assertive, enthusiastic, and energetic at the time of ovulation, and quieter, calmer, and more reserved around their period. Because I tend to overbalance on the enthusiastic, energetic side, Rachael asked quite seriously, "Do you *ever* get your period?" So much for sharing information before putting it into practice.

Women who accept the recurrent changes that are part of their physical and emotional nature can draw power from every phase of their monthly cycle. Watch your moods and the ways your priorities shift as you progress through the month. Make brief notations in your journal or your day planner of what you notice. Do this for more than one cycle so you can discern a pattern.

Once you have a grasp of how your cycles affect you, you can schedule discretionary activities accordingly. When it comes to obligations you're not free to schedule, you can at least arrange for whatever additional time, preparation, or moral support you need to make operating outside your natural rhythms less disruptive.

In addition to monthly hormonal fluctuations, a woman's life itself is made up of venerable cycles. Its three primary stages were traditionally referred to as that of the maiden, the mother, and the crone. Modern times have introduced further refinements. Girls reach puberty, for instance, long before they're ready to become mothers; and today's postmenopausal woman is the physical, sexual, and energetic antithesis of the geriatric state implied by the word *crone.*

Nevertheless, the spiritual overtones of these stages remain valid. As a maiden, we gain the knowledge we need for getting along in life. As a mother, or a woman at the age when motherhood is possible, we have the opportunity to share our knowledge with children, partners, clients, co-workers, and the world at large. As a mature woman, we can see our knowledge and life experience transformed into wisdom: wisdom to both keep and share, wisdom for life and wisdom for eternity.

That's pretty heady stuff when you're dealing with menstrual cramps or hot flashes, but these tribulations do have a certain initiatory element. When they fall in the category of "the only way out is through," you end up with a measure of courage and stamina you might not have come upon otherwise. When they inspire you to take greater responsibility for your own well-being, you find yourself both healthier and more empowered.

No woman can lead a charmed life without respecting her cyclic proclivities, both month to month and decade to decade. We are exquisite at every stage. Our challenge is to remember that, accept it as true, and attend to ourselves accordingly.

68.

STAND ON CEREMONY

Start giving yourself the blessing of ceremony by recognizing those that grace your life already.

Most people don't have time for lengthy retreats, sacred pilgrimages, or personal training with a guru. What we've got time for is living today: feeding the cat, going to work, driving a kid to the orthodontist, getting dinner on the table, finding some scrap of significant time to spend with our significant other. If we can accessorize such ordinary activities with a hint of ceremony, they become substantially less ordinary and more fulfilling.

A sense of ceremony enables you to grace mundane enterprises with the potential for deeper purpose. Reading a child a bedtime story (or, for that matter, reading *yourself* a bedtime story), buying fresh flowers every payday, making pancakes on Sunday morning—any of these can become rituals your interior being can expect and benefit from.

In a pragmatic way, such rituals simplify your life because they enable you to know, in some areas at least, what's coming, what to expect. At the same time, they can add a celebratory element to a routine that seems overly predictable and prosaic. Simple ceremonies drawn from daily life add color to your days without cluttering them.

Start giving yourself the blessing of ceremony by recognizing those that grace your life already. If you go to church or temple regularly, that's a worship ritual. If you meet the same friend for lunch the first Thursday of the month, that's a social ritual. If you make your famous shortcake every June when the first home-grown strawberries show up at the farmers' market, that's a seasonal ritual.

Before we were married, my husband told me that taking the ornaments off his Christmas tree was always sad for him. He said he wished he could have a multipurpose holiday tree that would stay on display all year, with the decorations changing to keep up with the calendar. So although we do a standard Christmas tree in the living room in December, we have a holiday tree in the playroom all the time. The ceremonial changing of its trimmings every couple of months is a rite that gives the kids—and their dad—great pleasure.

Your family history and your religious and ethnic background can be rich sources for personal traditions. Look at your friends' rituals as well. We often admire other people's ability to do with flair the same things we tend to muddle through. But no one has a patent on her ceremonies: let those of men and women you respect inspire yours.

The intentional, repeated, respected ceremonies that warm your heart also charm your life. A well-placed ritual here and there shows anyone who's watching—yourself most of all—that even in this seemingly haphazard world, some people are living on purpose.

69.

ALLOW FOR
MIRACLES

*Don't get too sophisticated
to be frequently amazed.*

The word *miracle* is unpopular with many pragmatic people. It conjures up the notion of some event that can have no rational explanation or, as one of my friends put it, "'Miracle' sounds like a TV preacher asking for money." It's the word I need to use here anyway: *miracle* according to Webster's second definition, "evidence of Divine power in human affairs."

When you look at miracles this way, you can see that we are swimming in a sea of them. Being in the right place at the right time, having precisely the item or the information you need, running into just the person who can help you solve a problem—you can see all these instances as "evidence of Divine power." When you do, life looks markedly less chaotic and more designed. When you notice these events for a time, you come to expect them. Once you expect them, they show up like stepping-stones along your path. People might comment on how lucky you seem to be, on how things so often work out well for you.

The three-part process for bringing such miracles into your life is this:

1. Look for evidence of divine power in your daily affairs.

2. Invite more of it in.

3. Be a catalyst for this power in other people's lives.

To look for indications of divine power, avoid taking things for granted. Really look at what you see—in nature, in people's faces, in human creations of art and technology. Don't get too sophisticated to be frequently amazed. You don't have to verbalize juvenile exclamations like "Wow!" and "Awesome!" but think them all you want.

Invite more divine power into your material world by expecting the best and doing the necessary footwork to birth those expectations. Act as if what you want were probable (refer back to Secret 34, "Study Method Acting"), and allow for the possibility that the true miracle may lie in an alternative outcome.

You can also lure miracles—or serendipity or right results; you can call them whatever you like—by speaking positively. Use words that are hospitable to whatever mobile miracle might be passing by. Even in something as insignificant as seeking a parking space, you may as well help on some level by saying, "I tend to find really good parking spaces" instead of "With all this construction, we'll never find a place to park."

(A fascinating aside here is that if you use the first statement and park three blocks from where you're going, you're likely to think, "This is great—only three blocks from the door." If you use the second, you're apt to complain, "Three whole blocks—as usual! I ought to keep hiking boots in the trunk.")

Finally, be a stimulus for other people's miracles. Encourage them to see their potential and life's potential. Remind them of the evidence of divine power you see in their lives already. Be a miracle provider by putting your own energy and generosity to work on another's behalf. And continue to allow for miracles, both minor and momentous, in your own life. That's how you show evidence of what can be.

70.

WORK A CHARMED JOB

The work we do can enhance our soul as well as our resume. Few of us had the benefit of an academic advisor or career counselor who recognized this vital dimension.

I always figured my livelihood would depend on a PC. I just thought that stood for Prince Charming. Instead, like many other women—and indeed like many other mothers—I work as well as making a home. When I love my work and feel satisfied by it, I know I'm in reasonably good shape spiritually. When I've been ignoring my deeper self, even having my dream job—which I do—seems like a burden. At those times, I don't want to be a writer anymore. I fantasize about being a Chanel lady in the cosmetics department at Sak's.

It's tough to live a charmed life if the work you do doesn't play some part in it, especially because work takes up so much of our time. Employed women ushered in today's female time crunch. Women who had been filling twenty-four hours as homemakers and mothers added eight hours of work and an hour or two of commuting. The phrase "working mother" came into common usage. Its definition: "a human female constantly engaged in some form of labor."

There is enough of the work ethic in us that all this working looked noble and right, so everybody joined in. Working women without children started working longer and harder. Housewives ceased to exist. Those who didn't enter the work force changed their job description. As "at-home moms," they were to involve their children in every sport, art, and enrichment activity a middle-class suburb could generate. Somebody had to do the driving. Voilà!—a way to stay home and be overwhelmed too. Talk about having it all.

Somewhere in the whirlwind of keeping busy, earning our keep, and expressing our talents is a concept the Buddhists call *right livelihood*. The work we do can enhance our soul as well as our resume. Few of us had the benefit of an academic advisor or career counselor who recognized this vital dimension. The result is that too many people do jobs they can perform but don't love. There are ways to change this. Among them:

Take a flying leap of faith. What would it take for you to work for yourself? Or to get a job in a field you find endlessly fascinating? Or to do something you believe in so thoroughly you'd do it for nothing if you could? Brainstorm your possibilities. With sufficient patience and planning, you probably *can* open the restaurant you've always wanted. Or go back to school. Or stop being an accountant and become a full-time masseuse or a full-time mommy, even if your accountant buddies will think you've lost your mind. Maybe you have, but losing your mind and finding your heart is a pretty good trade.

Make a living the easiest way possible, and live your dreams after hours. People who make this choice may give up an impressive job title, but they get energy to spare for art or music or wielding a hammer with Habitat for Humanity. My friend George knew this secret. George worked in maintenance.

Acquaintances were always telling him, "If you'd just get a degree, you could stop pushing that broom." But his friends knew the real story. George was a filmmaker, film collector, and film connoisseur. "Pushing that broom" made it possible for him to pursue the passion that made his life rich and meaningful.

See the work you do as spiritual practice. Do the job you do right now in a way that reflects what you believe in. (The reverse of this is Miss Polly Purity, who seems all innocence and caring but is actually pitting co-workers against one another and turning the office upside down.) If your beliefs are worth living by, they're worth working by. This will bring a higher degree of integrity to your job and ultimately to your company. You can also use the precepts on which you base your life to help you through the inevitable setbacks at work.

See the forest and *the trees.* Too many people go to work, put in their time, and go home. But if you keep sight of the bigger picture, your work instantly becomes more meaningful. What's your bigger picture? Beyond buying the groceries, why are you working? Is it to put your children through college? To express yourself? To help other people? Remember this when the little things are especially irritating.

Discover the inner aspect of the work you do. Every task is part of something bigger. At the core of all honest work is service, providing people with something that makes their lives a little better. When you see it that way, God becomes your employer regardless of who signs your paycheck.

71.

WALK

*However you fit walking into your day, choose an appealing
route, wear shoes so comfortable Mercury would trade his
wings for them, and fuel your walks with water. . . .
Water, like walking, is basic, grounding, and healing.*

To see where you're going and know where you've been, walk. To
lift your spirits, tone your muscles, and touch the earth, walk.
To get a grip on what really matters and put problems in perspective, walk. "We have mostly luxury problems anyway," a friend
told me once. He happens to be an avid walker.

Having an automobile in the driveway can make walking
seem like a laborious way to get anywhere, but choosing to walk
as often as possible can be a very practical component of a
charmed life. Many of the other charmed life suggestions can be
incorporated into walking: quiet time, slowing down, noticing
details, increasing your vitality, and keeping pace with the seasons. Admittedly, walking is easier in certain locales than others
because of the area's climate, the topography, and some town
planner's opinion on the relative importance of sidewalks. When
my husband and I chose the house we did, a major factor was its
proximity to restaurants, shops, and services. With ample reasons
for people to walk, the neighborhood stays lively and safe.

If you're a resident of hiking country like the Pacific
Northwest, nothing is more natural than taking off on foot down

some trail or another. And if you live in a walking city like New York or London, everybody walks and there's so much activity on the street you'd have to be sleepwalking to get bored. In some other places, it can take both discipline and creativity to incorporate walking into your day. Brainstorm in your journal or with a friend, ways to get more walking in your life.

What can you walk to from where you live? The dry cleaner? The post office? The bank? Church? What walking could you do downtown before work or on your lunch hour? If you can come up with satisfactory answers to these questions, you'll be able to do the most obvious kind of walking, the kind that has an end point.

Lacking this, you can simply take a walk. Having a dog is as good as having a destination. Walking with your true love is great for bonding as well as for both your hearts. Walking with a friend is an imaginative alternative to meeting for lunch. Walking in solitude is unparalleled for collecting your thoughts, mending your mood, and observing nature, architecture, and people in a way you never would from an automobile. It's like trading in your balcony ticket for a front-row seat.

You can even do a moving meditation by walking more slowly than usual and synchronizing your breathing with your steps. One woman I know does thirty minutes of fitness walking before breakfast and fifteen minutes of walking meditation with her husband after dinner. In less time than she used to spend getting to the gym, she takes care of her body, her soul, and her relationship.

However you fit walking into your day, choose an appealing route, wear shoes so comfortable Mercury would trade his wings for them, and fuel your walks with water. I've read the bizarre statistic that Americans drink less water than soda. But our bodies are nearly 70 per cent water—H_2O, noncarbonated, and with no artificial sweetener or phosphoric acid. Water, like walking, is basic, grounding, and healing. They go together. They'll keep you in shape and on target.

72.

ENROLL IN
RENAISSANCE 101

*The more things you can do, the more you'll have to delight
in. Don't second-guess your choices ("Can I knit and still be
a feminist?"). Be proud of all you can do.*

My car wouldn't start and my daughter needed a ride to a dress
rehearsal in the far-off suburbs that public transportation has
never visited. No one I called was free for chauffeur duty, but my
neighbor Mary said, "Just borrow our car. You can drive a stick,
can't you?" Yes! I could indeed shift gears. I could get my daughter to rehearsal. My expertise would save the day.

I was elated by my mastery of a manual transmission because
I knew it was one of the few miscellaneous competencies I'd man-
aged to acquire. Like most of us, I was educated for earning
money and reciting facts. This background can foster brilliant
careers and champion players of *Trivial Pursuit*. It does not often
make for a magical life, however, and when you're stuck by the
side of the road with a flat tire, it's completely worthless.

We think well of women who don't just *know* things but can
actually *do* things. This may well be the key to the popularity of
such diverse role models as Martha Stewart and *Dr. Quinn,
Medicine Woman*. My friend Jan can do things, too. She can grow
vegetables and preserve them, play the piano and sing, sew cos-

tumes, speak Spanish, write poetry, and craft wooden toys and beaded jewelry that people actually pay money for. And Jan doesn't stop with driving a standard transmission: she can drive a truck.

I am intrigued less by Jan's specific accomplishments than by her overall able-ness. A personal resume like hers has pride and power in it. Mine was quite a bit shorter the day I borrowed that car. I could type with all my fingers, wrap lovely packages, get by in the kitchen, and, as long as I kept most verbs in the present tense, speak French. It was a reasonable start.

What does your abilities list look like? What can you do that makes you feel adept at living on this planet? Can you bake bread? Read music? Pitch a tent? Paint a room? Train a puppy? Organize a closet or a file or a household?

Write down what you can do now, give yourself credit for it, and promise yourself you'll expand your catalog of capabilities. You can resurrect an old talent (that easel is in the attic somewhere) or learn something new. A good exercise is to commit to learning two new things: one you know you'll love and one you think you won't. (Right now I have tango lessons in the first category and expanding my computer skills in the second.)

When you learn to do something, as opposed to simply learning about something, you almost always end up liking it. The self-esteem boost that results is real and lasting. I'll bet you can still remember where you were when you first learned to tie your shoes—and how much you were beaming.

The more things you can do, the more you'll have to delight in. Don't second-guess your choices ("Can I knit and still be a feminist?"). Be proud of all you can do. With every proficiency you chalk up, you become increasingly independent and secure. You stop defining yourself by your job title and start seeing yourself as a Renaissance woman—capable, multifaceted, and in the driver's seat.

73.

ACCEPT THINGS
AS THEY ARE

*Happiness comes from accepting the present situation,
whether it's something you wish to savor as long as
possible or change as quickly as you can. Neither is
possible without acceptance as the starting point.*

There are two ways to be happy: getting what you want, and wanting what you've got. The second is more reliable and almost always lasts longer. Wanting what you've got doesn't mean settling for less than you deserve or desire. It means being content moment to moment by accepting things as they are.

People who do not learn the art of acceptance cannot be happy, even when they do get what they want. Happiness comes from accepting the present situation, whether it's something you wish to savor as long as possible or change as quickly as you can. Neither is possible without acceptance as the starting point, because without acceptance, you are living on the periphery of your life. There at the edges, you can't fully enjoy the good stuff or do anything about the rest.

One reason acceptance is so hard to come by is that we're programmed to work toward a better life. This isn't a bad thing, but it can get in the way when the yearning for more keeps us from noticing all that's here already. Bittersweet laments like "I didn't realize how good we had it" and "I didn't really appreciate her until she was gone" are testaments to the all-too-common sentiment that if life could be rewound and taped over, we'd do it a whole lot better.

During my ten years as a single mom, I was so focused on making us a real family that I didn't realize I had actually done precisely that. Shortly after I remarried, I commiserated with my friend Tess about all the adjustments that seemed called for. "Life was so easy before and I didn't even know it," I told her. "Those were precious times you had," she said. (I do like it when somebody agrees with me.) "But these are precious times too. It just may take you a while to see that." (The down side of having friends who will tell it to you straight is that they sometimes do.)

Tess showed me how crucial it was to accept the past as it had been and the present as it was then unfolding. Otherwise, I would lose the irreplaceable. Accepting the beauty of my new life didn't excuse me from making those needed adjustments; it just kept them from seeming so hard. Besides, by then I was happy. Before acceptance, I hadn't given happiness the time of day.

Anyone in the market for a charmed life would be wise to practice acceptance in these areas:

Self—height, age, marital status, temperament, appearance, state of health, and genetic predispositions included.

The past—family history, assorted hurts, disappointments, and regrets, plus all the good-old-days stuff about how great things were two (or twenty) years ago.

The present—location, occupation, income, and who is around at the present time and who isn't.

Other people—even those who don't accept us, and especially those closest to us whose lives we are experts on.

Uncontrollable circumstances—death, taxes, the weather, the salaries of professional athletes.

Whatever comes—joy, sorrow, change, loss, surprises, and miracles, to name a few.

With acceptance of these comes energy and clarity. Acceptance puts you squarely in the center of your real life, where you have substantial say as to the direction it takes. When you accept everything, you're suddenly free to change some things. Acceptance is the ideal state to be in if you're hoping to run into contentment. Every so often, even bliss stops by.

74.

TRUST YOUR INSTINCTS

*Sometimes the only difference between a woman who has
created a charmed life for herself and one who hasn't is
that the first was brave enough to trust her instincts.*

You know more than you think you know. We all do. Sometimes
the only difference between a woman who has created a charmed
life for herself and one who hasn't is that the first was brave
enough to trust her instincts. Lots of words describe these: *intuition, gut reactions, funny feelings, sneaking suspicions.* Whatever
you call it, we have, in addition to our senses and our intellect, a
way of knowing that is direct, dependable, and as natural to
human beings as having an opposing thumb.

There is nothing weird about your intuitive capacity, and you
don't need the theme from *The Twilight Zone* playing in the background in order to use it. The only reason such a caveat is even
necessary is that we live in a culture that, thanks to Descartes and
rationalism, has given short shrift to anything that can't be dis-
sected in a laboratory.

The newer sciences are changing this. Psycho-neuro-
immunology (I put in the hyphens because no word should be
that long unless it's in Welsh) has revealed how potently the mind
affects the body. Quantum physics reads less like Newton than
Meister Eckhart and Teilhard de Chardin. Scientist and philoso-
pher Gary Zukav devotes a chapter of his book *The Seat of the Soul*

to intuition, which he defines as "perception beyond the physical senses that is meant to assist you. . . . It serves survival . . . creativity . . . [and] inspiration."

What all this discussion amounts to on a personal level is that we're living at a time conducive to trusting our instincts. If you don't think yours are active or credible, it's probably because you haven't paid attention to them for a while. One sure thing about instincts is they're not noisy. This inner knowing tends to come in the form of a gentle nudge, a wordless whisper. If you don't make a point of being aware of it, you probably won't be.

Knowing this, pay some heed to the quiet hints that come from within you: a warning, an idea, an inclination to go one way or another. Don't dismiss these outright, or ignore them and lose them the way the memory of a dream can fade in the first minutes of morning.

On the other hand, exercise good sense. Until you become proficient at working with your intuition, you might confuse it with something else. "I just had a feeling I was supposed to buy a new car" could be solid instinct; it could also be self-serving rationalization. Bring your hunches to the attention of your logical faculties. Discuss them with someone whose opinions you value. Choose this person well. You want someone who has her feet on the ground, and who also relies on her own instincts and knows how to do it.

Refine your intuitive capacity by giving adequate attention to your spiritual self. Meditation helps a lot. So does looking for connectedness, even when separation is more readily apparent. Courting synchronicity is another invaluable aid. You do this by noticing coincidences such as two people recommending the same book, a friend calling at the moment you thought of her, or coming across the information you needed in some unlikely place like a bus ad or an infomercial.

Once you get into the habit of noticing helpful synchronicity, it will appear in your life more often. And once you get into the habit of listening for inner guidance, you'll get more of it.

75.

EMBRACE IMPERFECTION

Working on yourself is one thing.
Working yourself over is something else.

When you can accept your imperfections and be kind to yourself whenever you feel you haven't done something right, you'll feel a peace that incessant strivers seldom do. Far from making you a terrible person, having imperfections you admit to and work on can endear you to those who love you. Having imperfections also gives you a reason to hang around on earth and learn some more. Of course you'll take responsibility for yourself and your actions, but when it comes to the high drama of wallowing in remorse, pass.

We all have times when we disregard our needs, misuse our time, fall short of our goals, offend someone who passes through our lives, or even hurt someone close to us. We have to be humble enough to learn from our transgressions as well as our transformations. A reasonable response to missing the mark is to repair any damage done as best we can and go forward on a different path.

Working on yourself is one thing. Working yourself over is something else. Freud once asked in desperation, "What do women want?" I asked the same question of hundreds of women as I wrote this book. Karen Kelly, the editor of my book *Love Yourself Thin*, succinctly voiced the consensus: "Women today want to have fun, be happy, and still be in charge of their lives." We get that through a healthy commitment to our values, accepting life on its own terms, and taking a rain check on perfection.

Expect your growth to follow the two-steps-forward, one-step-back pattern. Everybody's does. The point is not to become a featured guest on *Lifestyles of the Serene and Exemplary*, because nobody's life-for-real is as impeccable as anybody's life-for-show.

What you can have (and what the suggestions you've been reading are intended to bring about) is a genuine sense of the divine in your life and a dependable feeling of peace because of it. You can find as much magic in a snowfall or a starry night as any five-year-old on the block. You can legitimately expect to establish a routine that provides adequate time for the people and projects that identify your life. You can eliminate imaginary limitations and use your energy to overcome real ones, which are much easier to deal with.

You can think and live so that your thoughts and actions attract serendipity the way putting out a bird feeder attracts robins and cardinals. You will never again look at some woman who seems to have everything and think, wistfully or enviously, "She leads a charmed life." You'll be too involved in living a charmed life of your own.

Resources for a Charmed Life

See *The Secret of the Golden Flower* (Secret 5), translated by Richard Wilhelm and Cary Baynes (Harcourt, Brace & Co., 1970).

For more information on *feng shui* (Secret 13), I recommend *The Western Guide to Feng Shui*, by Terah Kathryn Collins (Hay House, 1996).

When you're enlarging your world (Secret 17), you may wish to contact People to People International, 501 East Armour Blvd., Kansas City, MO 64110, an organization dedicated to creating international goodwill through travel programs and networking among people the world over.

Let your menus change with the seasons (Secret 18) with the exquisite, seasonal recipe book *Food for the Spirit*, by Manuela Dunn Mascetti and Arunima Borthwick (Daybreak Books, 1998).

If you're seeking to simplify (or "Complicate Selectively," Secret 20), the books by Elaine St. James are little godsends. I found *Living the Simple Life* (Hyperion, 1996) particularly useful.

A fascinating exploration of the connection between food and spirit (Secret 21) is *Feeding the Body, Nourishing the Soul*, by Deborah Kesten (Conari Press, 1997).

To further explore practical techniques for a bit of razzle-dazzle (Secret 22), see *Star Quality*, by Christen Brown (Ballantine Books, 1996).

A classic anthology on the Laws referred to in Secret 25 is *The Perennial Philosophy*, by Aldous Huxley (HarperCollins, 1990).

A book about making your whole house a sacred spot (Secret 27) is *Sacred Space*, by Denise Linn (Ballantine Books, 1995).

Extra help on growing through the hard times (Secret 35) may be found in *Good News for Bad Days*, by Father Paul Keenan (Warner Books, 1998).

Quoted in Secret 37 is *Care of the Soul*, by Thomas Moore (HarperCollins, 1992).

To form a spiritually oriented circle similar to the mastermind alliance discussed in Secret 39, see *Sacred Circles*, by Robin Deen Carnes and Sally Craig (HarperSanFrancisco, 1998).

In addition to Jerrold Mundis's book *How to Get Out of Debt, Stay Out of Debt, and Live Prosperously* (Bantam, 1990), helpful books on financial well-being (Secret 41) include *Don't Worry, Make Money*, by Richard Carlson (Hyperion, 1998), *Your Money or Your Life*, by Joe Dominguez and Vicki Robin (Viking, 1992), *Earn What You Deserve* (Bantam, 1996), by Jerrold Mundis, and *The Abundance Book*, by John Randolph Price (Hay House, 1996).

Talane Miedaner (Secret 44) is the author of an audiotape filled with fresh ideas for attracting the things you want. Her audiotape *Irresistible Attraction: A Way of Life*, can be ordered by calling 1–888–4–TALANE.

Listen with Your Heart, by Eileen Flanagan (Warner Books, 1998) is a lovely little book about seeking the sacred in romantic love (Secret 45).

For more information on the work of Charlotte Mason (Secret 48), read *For the Children's Sake*, by Susan Schafer MacCauley (Good News Publishers, 1984), or subscribe to Charlotte Mason Communique-tions, 4441 S. Meridian, Suite 221, Puyallup, WA 98373.

Valuable books on every aspect of becoming healthier (Secret 55) include *Perfect Health*, by Dr. Deepak Chopra (Harmony Books, 1991), and *Choose Radiant Health and Happiness*, by Susan Smith Jones (Celestial Arts, 1998). One way to join with others committed to healthy living is through the American Natural Hygiene Society, P.O. Box 30630, Tampa, FL 33630.

Delightful works on sanctifying the ordinary (Secret 56) include *Everyday Sacred*, by Sue Bender (HarperSanFrancisco, 1996), and *The Re-Enchantment of Everyday Life*, by Thomas Moore (HarperCollins, 1996).

Fine books dealing with the so-called mystical experience (Secret 59) are *A Most Surprising Song*, by LouAnn Stahl (Unity Books, 1992), and *The Way of the Mystic*, by Joan Borysenko (Hay House, 1997).

A source for nonelectric gizmos (Secret 60) is Leaman's Non-Electric Catalog, P.O. Box 41, Kidron, OH 44636–0041.

My book about home (Secret 61) is *Shelter for the Spirit:*

How to Create Your Own Haven in a Hectic World
(HarperCollins, 1998). And while we're on the subject, an
invaluable book if you're moving to a new house or a new city is
Will This Place Ever Feel Like Home? by Leslie Levine
(Dearborn, 1998).

The little books I mentioned as being on my desk while I
wrote "Come up with Quick Connections" (Secret 63) are
Midlife Awakenings, by Barbara Bartocci (Ave Maria Press,
1998), and *God Made Easy*, by Patrice Karst (Warner Books,
1997).

As you midwife dreams—your own and others'—(Secret
65), you may want to look into the work of "dream-
achievement expert" Marcia Wieder in her book *Doing Less and
Having More* (William Morrow & Co, 1998).

Literature by Tamara Slayton on female cycles (Secret 67) is
available through Womankind, P.O. Box 1613, Sebastopol, CA
95473.

The definitive book on right livelihood (Secret 70) is *Do
What You Love and the Money Will Follow*, by Marsha Sinetar
(DTP, 1989).

For a blending of fitness walking and meditative walking
(Secret 71), see *The Spirited Walker*, by Carolyn Scott Kortge
(HarperSanFrancisco, 1998).

Intuition (Secret 74) is dealt with in detail in Gary Zukav's
The Seat of the Soul (Fireside Books, 1989).

You may write to the author, or to request guidelines for forming a *Charmed Life Study Circle*, at:

P.O. Box 3344
Kansas City, KS 66103
(Please include a stamped, self-addressed envelope.)

To discuss booking a presentation by Victoria Moran for your organization, please contact either of the following speakers' bureaus:

Five Star Speakers
Attn. Nancy Lauterbach
8685 W. 96th Street
Overland Park, KS 66212
(913) 648–6480, x202

or

Authors Unlimited
Attn. Arlynn Greenbaum
31 E. 32nd Street, Suite 300
New York, NY 10016
(212) 481–8484, x320